Money Skills For Teens Made Simple

A Guide to Empowering Teens to Create A
Financially Secure Future Through
Savings, Budgeting, Financial Planning,
Spending And Investing

Kemi Emmanuel

Contents

Contents

Introduction

Have you ever felt overwhelmed when someone talks about budgets, savings, or investments? Believe me, I have experienced that too. Despite being surrounded by the world of finance in my younger years, I struggled to keep up with basic money matters when I set out on my own. It was a shock when I realized that my lack of financial knowledge as a teenager did not just go away; I had to learn everything the hard way. Research backs up this personal experience and shows that teenagers who are equipped with financial knowledge tend to have a more stable and prosperous financial future and make good decisions about debt, investments, income, and savings later in life. They can live fulfilled lives and even retire early because they have income and finances that set them up for life. Research also shows that children who start learning about personal finance from age 7 get a better grasp of the various concepts. I know that, as a teenager, the last thing you think about is what retirement looks like. Well, I thought like that too, and now I find myself nearer to retirement age than I ever expected!

Allow me to introduce myself: I am a graduate of business administration with a focus in finance and an entrepreneur who has started several businesses, including education and property management. More importantly, as a mother, teacher, and nurse who has worked extensively with young people, I am passionate about empowering young people like you with the essential financial knowledge they need.

This book is crafted with a clear goal: to equip you with vital financial knowledge and skills that will help you throughout your life. You will find that this guide is full of practical exercises to encourage you to get involved, expert advice for parents, engaging visual content, and direct links to invaluable resources. We explore everything from the basics of opening a bank account to the complexities of digital banking and online investing, all tailored to fit into your digital intelligence lifestyle.

What sets this book apart is its commitment to clarity and engagement. Using visuals, complex financial concepts are broken down into understandable sections. You'll read real-life success stories and even take part in interactive quizzes and practical exercises that ensure you actively participate. An activity book created specifically to build your knowledge and enable you to practice your understanding has been developed to accompany this book. As they say, practice makes perfect.

A unique aspect of this journey is the involvement of your parents. This book encourages open conversations about money within your family, promoting a holistic approach to learning that includes those closest to you. Studies show that open and collaborative financial discussions with family and friends can significantly improve teenagers' financial literacy.

The tone of this book is friendly and conversational. Consider this book a conversation with someone who gets it — no jargon, no lectures, just straightforward advice and support.

This book is an invitation to embark on a journey towards personal financial independence and financial literacy. By the end of this book, you will not only understand how money works, but you will be ready to apply what you have learnt. Throughout this book, you'll embark on a transformative journey to master the art of effective saving, make smart investment decisions, ensure wise spending approaches, and strategically expand your financial resources through multiple streams of income. This comprehensive approach will enable you to build a solid foundation for your financial future and thrive and achieve your long-term wealth goals.

Finally, I urge you to consider the charitable side of finance by using a portion of your income to support causes that are close to your heart and to embark on supporting the faith which you believe in. This act of generosity not only helps those in need but also enriches your own life and fosters a culture of giving that develops along with your financial literacy.

So dive in, engage with the content, and apply what you learn. The more you engage, the more you will benefit. We'll put you on a path where you can earn and manage money and make a difference with it. Welcome to a world where Personal financial knowledge meets real-world applications — I am so excited for you to embark on this journey. You will excel here, and I know you will!

Chapter1:
Building the Foundation

Hello everyone! Let's start with a little story. Remember that one time when you got some money for your birthday and had to decide whether to spend it right away or save it for something big? Maybe you wanted to buy yourself the latest smartphone or the latest Nike sneakers. This is just a small glimpse into the adventures of money management, and believe me, it gets even more interesting. I must point out that what matters to us as teenagers depends on what spectrum of the teenage line you are on, and I mean whether you are at the start of your teen years aged 13/14 or at the latter part of your teen years aged 18/19.

In this chapter, we will break down some of those tricky financial terms that adults throw around like confetti and show you how to understand them using language and examples that speak directly to you. No more feeling lost in translation! We will build your personal financial knowledge from the ground up, starting with the basic terms. It's about giving you the tools to not only understand your financial journey but to take control of it.

1.1 Decoding Financial Jargon with simple language

Let's dive right into the sea of "financial jargon" and fish out some common terms by breaking them down in simple lingo to make it all as digestible as a slice of your favorite pizza.

Translate Common Financial Terms

First, let's talk about "assets." Simply put, assets are the cool stuff you own that can be worth money. Think about your gaming console or iPad, for example. These aren't just fun gadgets; they're assets because they have value.

Next, we have "liabilities". These are pretty much the opposite. Liabilities are what you owe, e.g., if you promised to pay a buddy back for covering your movie ticket. It's like a debt that hangs over your head until you pay it off.

Now for "interest." Let's say you lend a friend $10, and when he pays you back, he gives you $12 instead. The extra $2? That's interest! That's what you earn when you make your money available to someone else for their use for a period.

Finally, "investments" are like a tiny money seed planted in something that can grow into more money, such as when you start your own small business or put money into a savings account that grows over time.

Activity 1
Interactive Glossary Creation

Why not create your own financial glossary? Pick up a notebook or use a digital app to jot down these terms along with your definitions of financial terms you stumble upon throughout this book. It's fun! Use your own words or make doodles to help you remember. This personalized glossary will be your guide when you come across new terms that might appear confusing throughout this book.

Use Sample in Fig 1

GLOSSARY OF TERMS

Fig 1

Financial Name	Term	Date	Meaning

Use Real-Life Scenarios

Let's just apply this, shall we? Imagine you have $300. You can either upgrade your phone now (and spend your fortune) or invest the money in a photography course (an investment that could earn you more money from photography jobs in the future). Each decision you make changes your financial future in its own unique way. Choosing between instant gratification and long-term payoff is a classic personal finance decision.

To conclude this section, how about testing your new knowledge? I've put together some flashcards and short quizzes that you can print out (see the section at the back of this book). They challenge you to match terms with their definitions and even use them in scenarios. It's a fun way to make sure you really understand these concepts.

And just like that, you've built a solid foundation of financial knowledge. By translating the jargon into your language and seeing how it fits into real-life situations, you will be well on your way to making informed personal financial decisions. Whether it's how to spend your birthday money or plan your first big investment, understanding these basics will put you in control. Keep your glossary up to date, and feel free to refer back to these quizzes anytime you need a quick refresher. Remember, every great financial expert started out as a beginner, just like you. Let's keep that momentum going as we cover more financial basics in the next few sections!

1.2 First Steps in Financial Literacy: What Every Teen Needs to Know

Understanding money isn't just about being able to afford the latest gadgets or having the means to hang out with friends whenever you want; it's about creating the conditions for a life of freedom and choice. Imagine being able to go to college, start your own business, or travel the world. These aren't just dreams; they can become reality if you understand money management. When you know how to manage your money, you can make smart decisions that will keep you debt-free and help you on the path to realizing your dreams. It's about more than dollars and cents; it's about understanding the value and power of money.

Let's look at the basic financial principles. These are: Earning, Saving and Investing, Borrowing and Spending. Each of these areas is a building block of financial literacy.

- **Earning**: Whether it's with a part-time job, an allowance, or money from odd jobs like babysitting or mowing the lawn, earning is your first step into the financial world. Every dollar you earn opens up new opportunities.

- **Saving**: This isn't just about putting money aside for a rainy day but also about preparing for future needs and wants. Whether you're saving money for the latest smartphone or tablet or putting money aside for your college education, saving is basically about securing your future.

- **Investments**: Although it may sound like something only adults do, young people can invest too. It can be as simple as investing in your own education through courses or as complex as investing in the stock market.

- **Spending**: Wise spending is just as important. It's about making decisions about how you use your money. Whether you decide to go for a meal with friends or save up the money for a concert, how you spend your money affects your financial situation.

- **Borrowing**: whether you are borrowing money from a friend to buy concert tickets, borrowing money to pay for a major purchase, or using credit cards for everyday purchases, you may find that you are borrowing money for yourself, and the decisions you make here can lead you into debt, which can have a negative impact on your financial future.

These principles play a crucial role in your current and future financial wellbeing, forming a complex network that determines your overall financial outlook.

Now, think about your daily financial decisions. Each decision, no matter how small, has an impact on your finances. Take, for example, the decision to buy lunch every day instead of packing it. A store-bought lunch could cost you $5 a day, which adds up to $25 a week or about $100 a month. Packing your lunch, on the other hand, might only cost you $2 a day. You can put the money you save toward savings or an investment. Over time, these small savings add up and can greatly improve your financial well-being.

To satisfy your financial curiosity, immerse yourself in the world of financial knowledge. There are a variety of apps, websites, and books designed specifically for you. Apps like **"Snoop"** (*money saving app*) help you track your spending and savings, while websites like Investopedia offer a wealth of articles that break down complex financial concepts into easy-to-understand information. Books, especially those designed to help teens manage money, can give you a solid foundation of financial knowledge. Explore these resources, and don't hesitate to ask your parents or teachers questions. The more you learn now, the better equipped you'll be to make smart financial decisions in the future.

1.3 Setting Up Your First Budget: A Guide for Teens

Imagine you have a certain amount of money available each month— - perhaps from your pocket money, a part-time job or a mixture of both. The challenge now is to figure out how best to use that money. And this is where the budget comes in. Think of a budget like a game plan or blueprint for your money. It's a plan that helps you manage your money in a way that strikes a balance between the fun things, like gaming, movies or hanging out with friends, and the less fun but necessary things, like saving for college or even a car.

The goal isn't just to limit your spending but to make sure you are spending your money wisely and getting the most out of every dollar. This means thinking about what's really important to you and finding the right balance between your wants and your needs. It is important to differentiate between your wants and your needs. Your needs are generally things you need, like food, clothing or shelter, while wants are the extra things we like to have or do but aren't essential, like games or going to the movies with friends! Don't get me wrong, as a teenager this is an important part of developing your social skills but being wise about this can make a whole world of difference to your personal finances.

A simple way to manage your budget is the 50/30/20 rule, which is very handy for keeping things simple. Here's how it works: 50% of your income should be spent on necessities — things you absolutely need, like groceries (if you contribute to shopping) or transportation costs. 30% is spent on wants—things that are fun, like new games, clothes or things to do with friends. The last 20% is set aside for savings or debt repayment, which may not sound exciting but is crucial to your future financial health.

Let's say you earn 100 dollars. Using the 50/30/20 rule, you would allocate 50 dollars to things like your cell phone bill or travel expenses, 30 dollars to a restaurant or that new video game you want to have, and 20 dollars to your savings. This framework can really help you prioritize and see where your money is going, which is especially useful if your income sources aren't as consistent.

To help you stick to this budget, there are some fantastic tools and apps designed specifically for people like you. **Apps like "Monefy", "Goodbudget", "Easy Budget", and YNAB (You Need A Budget)** are great because they do a lot of the work for you. They automatically categorize your spending, help you set goals, and even track your progress. These tools are ideal for keeping track of your finances without feeling overwhelmed. They can notify you when you've almost reached the limit in a category or congratulate you when you've reached a savings goal, making the whole process much more interactive and—dare I say it—a bit of fun too.

Now, let's talk about real-life examples because it's always easier to understand something when you have something tangible in front of you. Imagine two friends, Alex and Casey. Alex gets $200 a month from a part-time job, and Casey gets $150 from pocket money and odd jobs. They both want to save up for a concert ticket that costs $75 and is available in 2months. Alex decides to apply the 50/30/20 rule, meaning he spends $100 on necessities like phone bills and transportation, $60 on wants like snacks and movies, and puts $40 into his savings account. On the other hand, Casey has not set a clear budget, spends $100 on a new pair of sneakers or handbag, and spends $30 on a restaurant meal. She only has $20 left over, which she decides to save. By the concert date, Alex has successfully saved enough for the ticket, while Casey has too little money and can't afford to go. This example shows that a budget—and sticking to it—can greatly impact what you can do with your money.

To get a better visual understanding of how budgeting works, there are numerous YouTube channels dedicated to financial literacy and budgeting tips. Channels such as "The Financial Diet", "Nate O'Brien", "Finance Education", "Studyquill", etc., offer practical advice and step-by-step instructions on how to create a budget, which can be very helpful, especially for beginners. They break down complex concepts into easily digestible information that is informative and engaging.

It's important to know that creating a budget isn't about limiting yourself — it's about making your money work effectively so you can enjoy your life without financial stress. Tools and apps can help you do this, but the biggest part is your understanding and commitment to sticking to your budget. Whether you're saving for something big or just trying to manage your day-to-day expenses, having a plan and the tools to do so can make all the difference. Keep exploring new avenues, adjusting your budget as needed and watching how your smart money management opens new opportunities for you.

Activity Two
Try creating a personal budget by identifying how much you intend to spend for your needs and wants and how much you intend to save. Remember your savings is a form of investment and you can receive additional money for keeping your money in a savings account. We would look further into this as we go along.
You can use the personal budget template in Fig 2

Monthly Budget

Month: Year:

Income	Budget	Actual
TOTAL		

Debt	Budget	Actual
TOTAL		

Expenses	Budget	Actual
TOTAL		

Flexible Expenses	Budget	Actual
TOTAL		

Notes:

Fig 2

1.4 Understanding Money Inflows and Outflows: A Visual Guide

Think of your financial life as a bustling city where money comes in and goes out through different streets and avenues. It's a dynamic place, and the flow of traffic — your money — needs to be carefully managed to avoid congestion and keep things running smoothly. To visualize this, you can think of diagrams and flowcharts that clearly show the paths your money takes. For example, a simple flowchart could illustrate how the money from a part-time job or pocket money comes in and then branches out into different expenses such as food, entertainment and savings as outgoings. These visual representations are beautiful to look at and serve as practical tools to make abstract financial concepts more concrete and understandable.

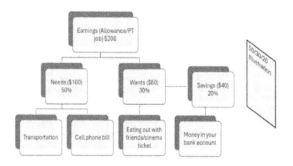

Let's look at a real-life scenario with Jamie, a sophomore in high school who just started her first part-time job at a local bookstore, earning $150 every two weeks. Jamie's goal is to save up for a new laptop by the end of the year, which costs $600. She decides to track her money inflows and outflows to better plan her spending and savings. Jamie's inflow is a manageable: $300 a month from her job. The outflow, however, is more varied. She spends $70 each month on transportation and cell phone expenses, $60 on dining out with friends, and $20 on her cell phone bill. After these expenses, she can save $150 a month if she sticks to her budget.

By analyzing her financial decisions using a chart, Jamie realizes that if she reduced her restaurant spending from $60 to $40, she could increase her savings to $170 per month, which would help her reach her goal faster. This visual representation helps Jamie see the impact of her spending habits on her savings goal and makes it easier for her to decide where to adjust her spending.

Activity 3

To deepen your understanding, try mapping your own money inflows and outflows. You can create a simple chart of income and expenses. Start by listing all your sources of income as inputs, e.g. allowances, birthday money or income from a part-time job. Then, track where the money goes each week or month, including expenses like snacks, movie tickets or savings for bigger goals. This activity isn't just about tracking but actively managing your money. By visualizing all of your financial activities, you can better make decisions that align with your financial goals and priorities.

Different choices in managing inflows and outflows can lead to different financial scenarios, and sometimes, the best way to understand this is to experiment with "what if" situations. What if you decided to walk or ride your bike instead of taking the bus? How much would you save, and how could this money be better spent on your goals? Or what if you found a way to earn a little extra money by tutoring or selling something you made? Adding these variables to your flowchart can reveal new possibilities and inspire you to be creative with your money.

Looking at your finances in a practical way can change the way you think about money. It's not just about numbers; it's about your choices and how they affect your financial future. So pick up some colored pens or use an app to draw your financial flowchart and start exploring the paths your money can take. Remember that every decision you make, no matter how small, affects the flow of money in and out of your life. By understanding and controlling these flows, you're taking active steps towards financial stability.

1.5 The Real Deal on Savings: Why Even Small Amounts Matter

Imagine the following: Every time you set aside a little money, whether from your weekly allowance or your grandparents' birthday money, it magically starts to grow on its own. Let's look at the power of compound interest, a concept that could become your new best friend on your financial journey. Imagine a scenario: Let's say you decide to save 10 dollars a week. That doesn't sound like much, but here's where it gets interesting. When you put that money into a savings account, it earns interest. This interest then earns interest as well. Over time, that initial 10 grows more than you might expect. It's like planting a single seed and watching it sprout into a whole garden full of flowers.

To make this even clearer, let's look at possible numbers. Let's say you put $10 into a savings account that earns 5% interest annually. After the first year, you don't just have your original $10; you have $10.50. If you leave the money in the bank, at the end of the second year, you'll no longer only receive interest on your original $10. You'll also receive interest on the $0.50 that your first $10 earned last year. So now you have $11.03. That may seem like a small change at first, but if you repeat the process, that money grows exponentially. If you continue this process, you'll build a future where your money works for you, not the other way around.

Why not take a moment to think about what you're saving for? Are you looking to buy the latest video game or a car when you turn sixteen, or are you saving for college expenses? Setting these sorts of goals is crucial because they give you a clear target and make saving feel less like a chore and more like a mission. For instance, if that video game costs $60, and you save $10 a week by cutting out chocolate bars and fast food, you will have enough money in just six weeks. Or maybe you're aiming bigger, like getting a car. If a used car costs $2000, and you save $50 every month, in less than three years, you'll be handing over cash for those car keys. These aren't just hypotheticals; they are realistic goals you can achieve with some planning and discipline.

Speaking of discipline, let's dive into some practical tips for effective saving. One simplest yet most effective strategy is to 'pay yourself first.' This means that before you spend money on anything else, set aside a portion of any money you receive—be it your allowance, paycheck from a part-time job, or a holiday gift—directly into your savings. It doesn't have to be a lot. It is essential to be consistent. Even small amounts add up if you're diligent about it. Another tip? Make it automatic. Use apps or bank settings to automatically transfer a small amount to your savings every month. That way, you won't be tempted to spend it because you won't even see it in your checking account.

Now, let's get inspired by some real-life victories. Take the story of Emily, a high school junior who saved up for her dream of backpacking across Europe. She steadily built up her travel fund by saving her tutoring money and birthday gifts and doing extra chores around the house for cash. It took patience and a lot of skipped outings with friends, but a year and a half later, she had enough to cover her trip. Or consider Marcus, who wanted a high-end computer for his graphic design projects. He saved small amounts from his part-time job at a café, and within a year, he was able to assemble his own PC, piece by piece. These stories aren't just about the end goals; they are about the sense of achievement and independence that comes from setting a goal, sticking to it, and seeing it through.

So, why do these stories matter? They show that saving isn't just about the future; it's about the choices and freedom that money can bring you today. Every dollar saved is a step towards independence, a buffer against unexpected setbacks, and a tool for achieving your dreams. The principles are the same whether it's a concert ticket or college tuition. Start small, stay consistent, and watch your money grow. And remember, every big saver started just like you, with a single dollar and a big dream.

1.6 Simple Tools to Track Your Spending and Saving

Let's explore some excellent tools for managing your money. Think of these apps and tools as your personal finance assistants—they keep an eye on your money so you can focus on more fun stuff, like planning your next big adventure or just hanging out with friends. We will look at a few popular ones, discuss what makes each special, and see which might best suit your style.

There's **You Need a Budget (YNAB)**. It's perfect if you like getting into the nitty-gritty of budgeting. YNAB helps you plan every dollar you earn, giving every bit of your cash a job, whether covering bills, going into savings, or just getting you through the weekend. It's great for getting a real handle on where your money goes, but it does come with a small monthly fee after a free trial, which might be a dealbreaker if you need more time to commit.

For a more straightforward option, there's **Wally**. This app is all about simplicity and visual appeal. It helps you track your expenses and provides insights into your spending patterns with bright, easy-to-read charts and graphics. It's convenient if you prefer a more visual approach to budgeting. Plus, Wally is free, which is always a bonus when trying to save.

Now, why bother tracking your spending and savings at all? Here's the thing: keeping a close eye on your finances doesn't just help you stick to your budget—it can actually help you save more. Understanding where your money flows daily illuminates spending patterns you might have overlooked. Those daily after-school snacks or frequent digital downloads can add up, and it's easy to underestimate their impact on your budget. By monitoring these expenditures diligently, you can adjust your spending habits, preparing you for a more advanced way of saving.

Setting up a tracking system may seem daunting, but it's simple. Let's walk through setting up a basic system using a budgeting app since it does most of the legwork for you.

Activity Four

Choose an app that fits your needs based on our previous suggestion. Download it, create an account, and link it to your bank account if the app requires it. Start by setting some primary goals in the app, like saving for a new bike or cutting back on eating out. The app should guide you through setting up categories for all your expenses so you can start tracking. Every time you spend money, log the expense in the app. Most apps will automatically categorize it for you, but it's good to check if something looks wrong.

Finally, make it a habit to review your spending and savings at least once a month. This is your monthly review routine. Look at where your money went, see if you stayed within your budget, and adjust as needed. You may decide to divert some money from dining out to your savings or spot a subscription you forgot about and can cancel. This regular check-in keeps you in control and helps you see your progress toward your goals.

I would like to point out that you need to be consistent to succeed with these tools. The more regularly you track your spending, the clearer your financial health picture will be. With a clearer picture, you can make better decisions, spot opportunities to save, and feel more confident about your finances. So, take some time to set up your system, choose the right tools for your needs, and start tracking. It's a small effort that can make a big difference in your financial future.

Chapter2:
Smart Money Management

W elcome back! Now that you've learned the basics of financial literacy, let's move on to one of the best tools at your disposal: budgeting. But it's not just any budget; it's about creating a budget that truly fits your teenage lifestyle. Whether you're saving for a concert ticket, managing money for a weekend getaway, or just want to make sure you have enough money for your next video game, a personal budget can make your money management smoother and more effective. Here's how to create a budget that feels less like a chore and more like a personalized plan for success.

2.1 Creating A Budget That Fits Your Teenage Lifestyle

Personalize Your Budget. First, your budget should reflect who you are and what is important to you. Start by writing down what you spend the most money on. Is it gadgets, clothes, snacks, or maybe books? What about your hobbies? Do you play sports, are you into art, or do you spend money on apps and games? And do not forget necessary expenses like school supplies. Once you have a clear picture, break them down into 'needs' (like transportation and school supplies) and 'wants' (like games or fashion). It's not about cutting out what you love but creating a balance that allows you to live out your interests without stress. I am sure your parents will cover many of your expenses when you are a teenager. However, it makes financial sense for you to start taking care of some of these needs yourself. This will prepare you to recognize the importance of taking responsibility for your needs.

You are a big fan of graphic novels. Instead of randomly buying books when you see them, set aside a monthly budget for your hobby. This way, you can continue building your collection without the guilt of overspending. It's all about making your budget fit your passions and responsibilities, turning it into a tool that helps you responsibly enjoy more of what you love.

Flexible Budgeting Techniques

As a teen, your income might come from different sources and can change monthly—maybe an allowance, a part-time job, or cash gifts during holidays. This is where flexible budgeting techniques come in handy. Two popular methods are the envelope system and zero-based budgeting.

The envelope system divides your cash into envelopes, each labeled with a category like 'Food,' 'Entertainment,' or 'Savings'. You spend only from the designated envelope, which helps you visually track and control your spending. On the other hand, zero-based budgeting is where every dollar you earn is assigned a job. At the start of the month, you allocate your total expected income to various expenses, ensuring that the income minus the expenses equals zero. It's a proactive way to manage your money, ensuring every dollar works for you.

Incorporate Fun Money

Remember, budgeting means cutting out only some of the fun. In fact, it's essential to allocate a specific category for 'fun money.' You want to make sure to take advantage of being a teenager. This is your go-to fund for small indulgences that make life enjoyable, like grabbing a latte with friends or an occasional movie night out. Setting aside a little fun money makes you less likely to feel deprived and more likely to stick to your budget. Think of it as your financial cheat meal; it keeps you on track without feeling restricted.

Budget Adjustments

Your budget should be adaptable and deal with any sudden surprises. One month, you earn more from a summer job or spend less on transportation than expected. Take some time each month to review your budget and adjust it. Did you find a new hobby? Are you spending more on outings? Reflecting on these changes helps you stay on top of your finances and ensures your budget grows with you.

For instance, if you start driving to college and need to budget for gas, you might cut back slightly on entertainment or eating out. Or if you got a raise at your part-time job, you could boost your savings or increase your spending a little on what matters most to you. Regular check-ins like this keep your budget realistic and practical, turning it into a dynamic tool that fits your evolving teen life.

Engaging in this active budget management keeps your finances under control. It enhances your understanding of how money works in real life. It empowers you to make informed decisions, reduces money-related stress, and builds a healthy relationship with money that can last a lifetime. So, grab that notepad or budgeting app and start sketching a budget that truly mirrors your life as a teen today (you can also use the template in Fig above). Remember, a well-planned budget isn't about restrictions; it's about making intelligent choices that amplify the fun and freedom money can bring into your life. Let's make your money work for you, not vice versa!

Activity 5

- Make a list of your income for the month.

- Identify the items you spend money on.

- Split them into wants and needs.

- Create an envelope for the different wants and needs identified.

- Create an envelope for savings.

- Review your budget at the end of the month.

- See if you have managed to stick to it or if you went over budget.

- Identify the areas in which you went over budget and reflect on why?

- Repeat the process for the next month but decide whether to increase your income to cover the areas where you went over budget or cut down your expenses in other areas.

- If you have a surplus and used only some of the money you budgeted for the items you identified, put the surplus cash in your savings envelope.

- Well done on completing this activity successfully!

2.2 Creative Savings Strategies for Short-Term Goals

When saving up for something special, like that epic gaming headset or a ticket to see your favorite band, your goal needs to be within reach. But with some clever strategies, you can make saving feel less like a chore and more fun. Let us explore some creative ways to keep your savings goals on track and inject a little excitement into the process.

Visual Goal Setting

First up, let's talk about keeping your goals in clear view. Have you ever thought about using a goal chart or a vision board? It works like this: you create a visual representation of what you're saving for—maybe it's pictures of a new bike, screenshots of a dream vacation, or a collage of festival tickets. Place it somewhere you'll see it every day, like on your wall or as the background on your phone. This isn't just about daydreaming; it's a powerful reminder of why you're saving in the first place. You can visually update your chart or board whenever you add money to your savings. Fill in a bar on a graph, add a sticker, or color in a section—it's satisfying to see your progress and helps keep the momentum going.

Micro-Saving Techniques

Now, let's get into the nitty-gritty of how to save. With micro-saving techniques, you can save small amounts without even noticing. Many banking apps now offer features that round up your purchases to the nearest dollar and stash the difference in savings. For instance, if you buy a coffee for $3.75, the app rounds it up to $4.00 and puts $0.25 into your savings. It might not seem like much, but it adds up quickly! Another method is setting up automatic weekly deposits—maybe just $5 or $10 into a savings account. It's like putting your savings on autopilot. You're slowly building up your funds without thinking about it too much, making it easier to stick to your savings goals.

Reward-Based Savings

Saving money doesn't have to be all work and no play. Setting up a reward system for yourself can make reaching your savings milestones feel like a victory. Let's say your goal is to save $200. You could break that goal into smaller chunks; every $50 saved will reward you. It could be a night out with friends, a new book, or a day off from chores. Choose rewards that motivate you but don't necessarily break the bank. This way, each milestone feels like a mini-celebration, keeping you motivated and focused on reaching your ultimate goal.

Group Savings Challenges

Lastly, why not make saving money a group effort? Team up with friends or family members with savings goals and challenge each other. You can set a joint goal or compete to see who can save the most each month. Create a chart to track everyone's progress and meet to discuss strategies and cheer each other on. Maybe throw a fun prize for the winner—a movie night hosted by the others, or the loser buys lunch. Turning saving into a social activity makes it more enjoyable. It introduces a bit of friendly competition to keep everyone on their toes. I decided to start the 1cent savings challenge with my 17year old daughter (see below table) to encourage her to save.

These creative savings strategies can make reaching your short-term financial goals more engaging and fun. Whether you're visualizing your progress, saving little by little, rewarding yourself for milestones, or competing with friends, each strategy offers a unique way to enhance your savings experience. So, pick the methods that resonate most with you, mix and match them as you like, and watch your savings grow towards your next big goal.

Activity

Try the 1-cent savings challenge Start by saving 1 cent on January 1st. Consider getting a piggy bank to help with this. On January 2nd, save 2 cents (i.e. add 1cent to every cent saved); on January 3rd, save 3 cents, and continue increasing your savings by 1 cent each day until December 31st. You will save 365 days to save. By the end of the year, you will have saved a total of $657.33 can be more in a leap year where February has 28days. You can see this as a form of compound interest! We shall discuss more about compound interest later in the book. It goes to show you that every cent counts. If you did not start on the 1st of the year, you can start by calculating how much should have gone into the jar by the day you start. For example, if you start on January 20th, put 2.10 cents in the jar, and then the next day, put in 21c, which you could have saved if you had started on January 1st. Try this and see how much fun it is watching your money grow. This is a great way to save towards a goal and to get into the habit of saving.

Step-by-Step Guide

- Set a target and determine how much you intend to save in the year, e.g., $657.33.

- Get a piggy bank or Jar for the money (you can also use an old empty container and cut a hole in the lid).

- Start saving between 1& 10c a day. The key is to add a penny to what you saved the previous day and save it the next day.

- You need to be consistent.

- If you miss one day, catch up the next day or the day after. If you are starting in the middle of the year, calculate how much you would have saved in that time, save the amount, and then continue from there.

- Consider making it a group challenge with family or friends

Reward yourself once you've achieved your goal.

1 cent Savings Challenge	
Month	**Amount**
January	$4.96
February	$12.69
March	$23.61
April	$31.65
May	$41.85
June	$49.65
July	$60.76
August	$70.06
September	$79.67
October	$86.25
November	$91.93
December	104.25
Total	657.33

2.3 Mastering the Art of Frugal Living Without Missing Out

Living frugally does not mean you cannot take advantage of the fun things in life. It's all about getting the most out of every dollar and finding creative ways to enjoy what you love without breaking the bank. Let's explore some smart spending habits that save money and keep you enjoying your favorite activities and items without feeling like you're constantly cutting corners.

One of the easiest ways to stretch your funds is to take advantage of student discounts. Many places like movie theaters, restaurants, and even online services offer discounts just for being a student. All you need is your student ID, and you can save anywhere from 10% to 50% on things you would buy anyway. It's like scoring an easy win every time you go out. Another great trick is to purchase second-hand. This could be anything from clothes to gadgets and even textbooks. Shops like thrift stores, consignment stores, or online platforms like eBay and Depop can be treasure troves for finding stylish clothes or tech at a fraction of the retail price. Remember, buying second hand saves you money and is a great way to support environmental sustainability.

Swapping goods and services with friends is another savvy way to live frugally. You're great at graphic design; your friend can teach you guitar. Swap lessons instead of paying for them. Or organize a clothing swap party where everyone brings items they no longer wear, and you can refresh your wardrobe for free. It's a fun way to get new-to-you items without spending any money, and it turns an otherwise regular weekend into an event to look forward to.

Investing in quality over quantity is another crucial strategy. It might seem counterintuitive when trying to save money but spending more on something that will last longer often means saving money in the long run. For instance, a slightly more expensive pair of shoes that will only wear out slowly can be a better investment than a cheap pair that needs to be replaced every few months. Think about cost per use: if a $60 pair of shoes lasts you a year of regular use, the price is less per day than a $30 pair that wears out in three months. Over time, investing in quality not only saves money but also helps reduce waste, making it a smart choice for your wallet and the planet.

DIY projects offer a fun and fulfilling way to save money while expressing creativity. Instead of purchasing expensive gifts, why not make them? Handmade gifts like knitted scarves, customized mugs, personalized greeting cards (lots of graphic software such as Canva are now available to aid with designing good quality cards which you can personalize) or even homemade candles offer a personal touch that can't be bought in a store and your family members or friends would appreciate the effort you put into it. It shows This reminds me of how much I used to love the presents my children gave me when they were younger because they were handmade, and they put so much effort into making it for me. I am sure this would be the same with your parents. Why not try making a picture of a member of your family or a group portrait using graphic software which creates drawings out of pictures and framing this as a memorable gift. Apps such as Snapchat can help with this. Upcycling clothing is another great DIY area to explore. With a few basic sewing skills, you can turn an old pair of jeans into a stylish tote bag or make a trendy crop top from an oversized shirt. Not only do you save money, but you also end up with something unique that's precisely to your taste. Plus, the satisfaction of saying, "I made this!" is priceless.

When hanging out with friends, plenty of low-cost or free activities are as fun as the pricier options. Instead of going out to eat, host a potluck dinner where everyone brings a dish. This way, you spend less on food and still have a fantastic time with friends. Outdoor activities like hiking, biking, or even a day at the beach offer great ways to stay active and have fun without spending much. And when you want to chill, why not have a movie marathon at home? Get some popcorn, grab snacks, and enjoy a day of movies or binge-watch a series together.

By adopting these frugal living strategies, you can save money while enjoying a prosperous life. It's all about making intelligent choices and looking for creative alternatives to the norm. Whether leveraging discounts, choosing quality over quantity, tackling DIY projects, or finding inexpensive ways to hang out with friends, living frugally doesn't mean giving up what you love. Instead, it means enjoying those things even more because you know you're making the most of every dollar. So embrace frugal living and watch how it opens up even more possibilities for fun and savings.

2.4 Apps and Tools to Simplify Your Financial Life

Managing personal finance as a teen can sometimes feel like trying to solve a Rubik's Cube—when you think you've got it, there's a new twist waiting for you. But here's the good news: tons of apps are designed to make managing your money as easy as streaming your favorite playlist. Let's explore some top financial apps that aren't just about keeping you on budget, they're about making your financial life more connected, secure, and fun.

First on the review list is "PocketGuard." As the name suggests, this app is all about guarding your pocket. It links to your bank accounts and automatically sorts your spending into categories, showing you how much money, you have in your pocket for everyday expenditures after setting aside funds for essentials and savings. What makes PocketGuard stand out for teens is its simplicity and clarity. It breaks down exactly how much money you can safely spend before your next allowance or paycheck. It is handy for ensuring you never overspend when you're out with friends.

Another great tool is "Acorns." Imagine if you could invest your spare change without even thinking about it—that's Acorns. This app rounds up your purchases to the nearest dollar and invests the difference in a diversified portfolio. You buy a snack for $1.75, and Acorns rounds it up to $2.00, taking that extra 25 cents and investing it for you. Over time, these little bits add up, and you're not just saving money; you're growing it. Acorns are perfect if you want to get a head start on investing without needing much money upfront.

Now, let's talk about how to link these apps safely with your bank accounts. Most financial apps require access to your banking information to automatically track your spending and savings. While this sounds scary, modern apps use advanced security measures like encryption to keep your data safe. Encryption is like a secret code that scrambles your information, making it unreadable to anyone who doesn't have permission to see it. Always ensure any app you use has robust security features and read reviews to see what other users say about its safety. Security is crucial, which brings us to another essential feature: two-factor authentication (2FA). Apps like "Mint" offer this, which you should absolutely use. Two-factor authentication adds an extra layer of security by requiring two forms of identification before you can access your account. Typically, you'll enter your password, and then the app will send a code to your phone that you need to enter. This means that even if someone gets your password, they won't be able to log in without also having access to your phone. It's a simple step that can significantly increase your accounts' security.

Lastly, let's dive into custom notifications, which can be a real game-changer. Apps like "YNAB" (You Need A Budget) allow you to set up alerts for almost anything. You can get notifications when you're close to reaching your spending limit in a category or achieving a savings goal. These reminders help keep you on track and make budgeting feel more like a game where you're always trying to beat your high score. Additionally, they can be customized to fit what you need—whether it's a nudge not to overspend on entertainment or a cheer when you save extra money in a month.

With these tools in your arsenal, managing your money can become less of a chore and a fun challenge. Whether you're keeping tabs on your spending, protecting your savings with top-notch security, or investing your spare change, an app can help. So explore these options, find what works best for you, and make your money management routine much brighter. Remember, in finance, being tech-savvy is your biggest asset.

2.5 Overcoming the Temptation to Overspend with Peer Pressure

Navigating the social waters of your teen years can be tricky, especially when managing money in social settings. The pressure to fit in, feel included, and keep up with the latest trends can tempt you to overspend. Whether it's splurging on that trendy outfit all your friends have or constantly dining out because everyone in your group does, these social triggers are natural and can quickly lead to a drained wallet. Let's tackle these challenges together and find ways to enjoy time with friends without compromising your financial well-being.

First off, identifying what triggers your overspending is crucial. This could be anything from a weekly outing with friends where everyone tends to splurge to feeling the need to buy the latest tech because all your peers have it. Or perhaps it's the influencer on your favorite social media platform showing off the latest fashion or gadgets. These triggers can often lead to impulse buys, which, let's be honest, feel great now but can lead to buyer's remorse later. Recognizing these triggers is the first step in managing them. You might start by tracking your spending habits for a month, noting instances where you felt pressured into spending. You'd be surprised how much this simple awareness can help curb unnecessary expenditures.

Now, onto building assertiveness—yes, it's okay to say no, and it's a skill that will benefit you beyond your teen years. Being assertive about your spending decisions can be challenging, especially if you fear it might make you look bad in front of your peers. But here's a little secret: being clear about your financial boundaries can earn you respect. It shows you're someone who is thoughtful and in control of your life. You can practice this by preparing responses for times you might feel pressured to spend. Simple statements like, "I'm saving up for something big," or "I have a budget I'm sticking to," said confidently, can do the trick. Remember, true friends will respect your decisions.

Planning for social spending can also save you from financial stress. If you know you have a weekend outing, plan your budget around it. Set aside a specific amount for these social expenses and stick to it. This might mean making some trade-offs elsewhere, but it allows you to enjoy your social life without the guilt of overspending. Additionally, why not suggest more budget-friendly activities? Instead of going out to a pricey concert, a movie night at someone's house, or a day at the park. Often, these low-cost hangouts can be just as fun, if not more, because they come without the stress of a hefty price tag.

Lastly, let's talk about the influence of advertising and social media. It's designed to make us want things we didn't even know we needed. Becoming savvy about these influences involves understanding marketers' tactics to attract young consumers like you. Next time you see an ad or a post urging you to buy something, take a moment to ask yourself why you want it. Is it because it genuinely interests you or because the marketing is convincing? Critically evaluating these messages can significantly reduce their impact on your spending habits, helping you make decisions based on your needs and desires rather than on a crafted image or fleeting trend.

By recognizing what triggers your overspending in social situations, practicing assertiveness, planning your social budget, and understanding the influence of marketing, you can enjoy your social life without letting it derail your financial goals. It's all about making conscious choices, respecting your financial journey, and not letting peer pressure dictate your spending. With these strategies, you can balance having fun with friends and maintaining your financial health.

2.6 Setting Financial Boundaries: A Guide for Teens and Their Parents

Navigating finances within the family unit can sometimes feel like walking a tightrope. It's about finding the right balance between independence, collaboration, privacy, and openness. One of the most effective ways to manage this delicate balance is through regular family financial meetings. Think of these as a safe space where everyone can share their thoughts about money matters without judgment. These meetings are your chance to set expectations, discuss financial goals, and establish clear boundaries about spending and saving. It's not just about numbers and budgets; it's about understanding each other's perspectives and working together towards common objectives.

Let's break down what these meetings look like. It could be a monthly sit-down at the kitchen table where you review your family budget, discuss upcoming expenses, or plan for big purchases. It's vital that everyone, including you as a teen, has a voice. Perhaps you're saving for a new laptop or planning for college expenses—this is your opportunity to express your needs and understand how they fit into the more comprehensive family finances. Also, use this time to celebrate successes, like reaching a savings goal or sticking to a budget, which can boost morale and encourage good financial habits.

Moving on to financial responsibility is crucial as you navigate your teen years. It's about more than just managing your money—it's about contributing to your household and learning the value of money through experience. If you receive an allowance or earn money from a part-time job, consider taking responsibility for certain expenses, like your cellphone bill or entertainment costs. This not only eases the financial burden on your parents but also teaches you the real-world impact of financial decisions. It's about making choices and dealing with the consequences, good or bad, which is a fundamental aspect of growing up.

As you age, privacy and control over your finances are key themes. While being open with your parents is important, having personal financial space is essential. This could mean having a savings account or using budgeting tools to track your spending independently. It's about building trust with your parents so that you can manage your money responsibly while also ensuring they respect your financial privacy. This can be a tricky balance to achieve, but it starts with open communication and mutual respect. Suppose you feel like your financial privacy isn't being respected. In that case, it's important to voice this calmly and rationally, explaining why this matters to you.

However, financial disagreements can arise despite the best plans, and knowing how to handle these situations is crucial. Conflict resolution skills come into play here. Start with open communication; express your views clearly and listen to the other person's perspective. Compromise is often crucial. You and your parents may disagree on how much you should save each month. You might propose a lower amount than they have in mind. Still, you could compromise by agreeing to review the amount after a few months to see if it can be adjusted. It's about finding a middle ground that respects your independence and your family's financial goals.

By engaging in regular financial discussions, taking responsibility for personal expenses, maintaining privacy, and navigating conflicts with understanding and compromise, you're laying down a strong foundation for economic independence. These skills are not just about managing money—they're about fostering relationships and building respect within your family. So, take these lessons to heart and use them to strengthen your financial and family bonds.

As we wrap up this chapter, remember that setting financial boundaries isn't just about rules and restrictions; it's about creating a framework within which you can explore, make mistakes, and grow. These boundaries allow you to learn about finances in a supportive environment. Next, we'll dive into more complex aspects of financial management, ensuring you're equipped to manage your money and make it grow and work for you. Remember these lessons, as they are the building blocks for the more advanced financial decisions and strategies we'll explore in the upcoming chapters.

Chapter3:
Banking and Credit Basics

Let's talk about something super important but often overlooked until you really need it: your first bank account. Think of it as your financial HQ, where your money hangs out, grows, and gets moving when required. Choosing where to open your first bank account might seem like another errand. Still, it's actually a big step towards independence. The right bank can be your ally, helping you manage your money more effectively as you navigate your teen years and beyond. So, how do you pick the best one? Let's dive into what you must look for to make an intelligent choice that suits your lifestyle.

3.1 Choosing Your First Bank Account: What to Look For

Types of Bank Accounts

First up, understanding the different types of bank accounts is crucial. This knowledge empowers you to make informed decisions about your money. You should know three main types: checking, savings, and student accounts. A checking account is like your everyday wallet but in digital form; it's where you'll deposit money you plan to spend soon. You can access your funds through checks (yes, they're still a thing), debit cards, or electronic transfers. On the other hand, a savings account is like a storage unit for your cash, ideal for the money you don't plan to use right away. Thanks to interest rates, it keeps your money safe and lets it grow a bit.

Then, student accounts are tailored specifically for teens and young adults like you. They often come with lower fees and offer perks like rewards for good grades or mobile apps designed for tech-savvy users. The choice you make on the type of account depends on what you need it for. A checking account might be the way to go if you're looking to manage daily expenses. But a savings account could be better if you're saving for something big or want to grow your money. If you can find an excellent student account, that might be the best of both worlds.

Fee Structures

Nobody likes fees, but they're a part of life when it comes to banking. However, knowing which bank you choose can help you minimize them. Different banks charge different fees for maintaining your account, using Automated Teller Machines (ATMs), aka cash machines, or if you accidentally spend more than you have (overdraft fees). These fees are charged when you spend more money than you have in your account, and they can add up quickly. It's essential to keep track of your balance and only spend what you have to avoid being charged fees. Some might even charge you for talking to a human teller or getting a paper statement. It's important to compare these fees because they can quickly eat into your savings if you're not careful.

When comparing banks, don't hesitate to ask for a complete list of fees, and think about how you use your bank to figure out which fees might apply to you most often. For instance, if you love using ATMs, select a bank with an extensive network of ATMs or one that reimburses ATM fees. This homework upfront can save you a lot of money and hassle later. Remember, there's no such thing as a silly question regarding your money. The more you know, the more confident you'll feel about your choice.

Banking Features

Now, let's talk about features. In today's digital world, features like mobile banking are not just lovely; they're essentials. Mobile banking apps can let you check your balance, transfer money, deposit checks, and even set budgeting goals from your phone. Alerts are another great feature, they can notify you of low balances, unusual activity, or upcoming payments, helping you stay on top of your finances without needing to log in constantly.

Also, consider whether a bank offers financial education resources. Some banks provide excellent tools for learning everything from the basics of budgeting to understanding credit. These can be incredibly valuable as you start your financial journey.

Bank Reputation and Accessibility

Finally, a bank's reputation and accessibility are crucial. A bank with a good reputation for customer service can be a lifesaver when you have a problem or a question. Online reviews, feedback from friends and family, and even awards or recognitions can give you a sense of a bank's reputation.

Accessibility is also crucial. Check if there are branches and ATMs near your home or school. Even though you can do a lot online, sometimes you need to talk to someone or use an ATM. And if you travel, consider whether your bank has branches or partner ATMs in other areas to avoid fees.

Choosing a bank might seem like a minor decision, but it can greatly affect your financial health. Take your time, research, and pick a bank that can grow with you and meet your current needs. Whether it's your first paycheck, car, or even your first house, the right bank can help you reach those milestones confidently and efficiently. Remember, this is about more than just storing your money; it's about making your money work for you. So, choose wisely, and take this first step towards financial independence with as much care as you'd select a smartphone or a laptop. After all, it will be one of the most important tools in your financial toolkit.

Activity

- Identify 5 banks around your area including online banks

- Research what accounts they have available and what interest rates they offer.

- Research how accessible they are and what the perks e.g. if they have ATMs where you can easily access your money.

- Find out if there is a charge for using ATMs.

- If you are in college, find out what accounts are available for students and what perks come with these accounts.

- Choose the bank that best meets your needs and go and open a bank account. You can go with your parents, siblings or any member of your extended family.

Remember this is the time to take advantage of these offers with several banks vying for new business from young adults like yourself. However, this might not be the case when you fully enter the world of work.

CONGRATULATIONS on opening your new bank account!

3.2 The ABCs of Credit Scores for Teens

Now, let's get into something that might sound super adult but is essential for you, too—credit scores. Imagine your credit score and see it as a financial report card. Just like your school report shows how well you're doing in your classes, your credit score is a quick summary of how well you handle your money, especially when it comes to borrowing and paying it back. But your score is a number instead of grades, usually between 300 and 850. The higher your score, the better you look to anyone who might lend you money, like banks or credit card companies.

Now, why should you care? Having a good credit score can ensure your financial life is much smoother. Want to get a car loan someday? Or a credit card? Or even rent an apartment? These can be easier and cheaper if you have a good credit score. For instance, with a good credit score, you might get a car loan with a lower interest rate, which means you pay less money over time. It's like having a VIP pass in the financial world—it can open doors and save you money through lower interest rates and better loan terms.

So, what affects your credit score? The biggest factor affecting your credit score is your credit history. This makes up about 35% of your score. This is whether you pay your bills on time. Just missing one payment can ding your score, so it's crucial to set reminders or automate payments if you can. Credit utilization is a fancy way of saying how much of your available credit you are using. It's a good rule of thumb to keep your usage under 30%. For example, if you have a credit card with a $1000 limit, try not to carry a balance of more than $300.

The length of your credit history is another significant factor impacting your credit score. This one's tricky for you as a teen since you're starting out. But here's an excellent tip: if your parents have good credit habits, you can ask to be authorized on their credit cards. This can help kickstart your credit history by piggybacking on their good credit standing. Remember, this only helps if the main account holder, in this case, your parents, uses credit responsibly. If they miss payments, it could hurt your score, too.

Checking your credit score is often like checking your school portal to see your grades. You can get a free credit report once a year from each of the three major credit bureaus; Equifax, Experian, and TransUnion at **Annual Credit Report.com**. This won't give you your score for free, but it will show you the details of your credit accounts, your payment history, current debts, and anything else affecting your score. It's essential to check this report regularly to ensure everything is correct. Errors are not a regular occurrence, but they happen and can mess up your score if you miss them.

Understanding and managing your credit score might seem daunting. Still, it's like any other skill, the more you practice, the better you get. Start simple. If you have a recurring bill, like a phone bill, pay it on time every month. Consider using a budgeting app that can remind you when bills are due. As you get more comfortable, you can dive deeper by getting a small credit card and using it responsibly to build your credit. Remember, good credit doesn't just happen overnight. It's built up gradually by consistently making smart financial decisions. Like in school, it's about showing up, doing the work, and staying consistent.

3.3 How to Use Credit Wisely: A Teen's Guide

Navigating the world of credit can feel like learning a new language. But once you get the hang of it, you'll see it's a powerful tool that can help you achieve some pretty cool goals. Understanding credit is about understanding trust. It's the trust banks and lenders put in you to borrow their money and return it within an agreed period. Think of it like borrowing a video game from a friend; they trust you'll give it back in good condition and on time. If you do, they'll likely lend you games in the future. You might find your friend less willing next time if you don't.

Credit comes in many forms, such as loans, credit cards, and lines of credit, and using it wisely starts with knowing the basics. One of the golden rules of using credit is paying off your monthly balances, especially for credit cards. Let's say you use a credit card to buy a new skateboard. If you pay off that purchase when your bill is due, you generally won't pay extra beyond the price of the skateboard. However, if you only make the minimum payment, the remainder of what you owe starts accumulating interest. Remember, credit card interest rates can be high, meaning that over time, you could end up paying much more than the original price of the skateboard.

Understanding interest rates and penalties is another crucial part of using credit wisely. Interest rates represent the cost of borrowing money, which can vary widely based on the type of credit product, the lender, and your creditworthiness. Lower rates mean you pay less overtime. Penalties are fees for late payments or breaches of your credit agreement terms. These can quickly add up, not to mention hurt your credit score, making future borrowing more difficult and expensive.

Credit isn't just for buying the latest gadgets or clothes; it can also be a pathway to making significant investments. For instance, many people use credit to buy a car, pay for college, or even start a business. Each scenario involves more substantial sums that might not be immediately accessible otherwise. But with greater borrowing comes great responsibility. Buying a car with a loan means committing to regular payments for several years. If you're using credit for college, you're investing in your future earning potential. However, it's still important to borrow what you need and understand the terms and conditions associated with the loan.

While credit can open doors, it also has pitfalls. One of the most common mistakes is overusing credit cards without a plan to pay off the balance quickly. Many people easily fall into the trap of thinking credit is extra money, but borrowing money comes with strings attached, mainly interest. Another potential pitfall is not paying your credit bills on time. Late payments can result in penalties and increased interest rates, negatively impacting your credit score. Over time, these can compound and lead to a cycle of debt that's hard to break.

Using credit wisely is about balance and understanding. It's about knowing when and how to use credit to your advantage and when to pull back. Once mastered, it's a skill that can provide financial flexibility and help you build a solid foundation for your future financial endeavors. Like any financial tool, the key to success with credit lies in education and responsible management. So take the time to learn as much as possible, stay vigilant about your spending habits, and always plan for the future. With these strategies, you're well on your way to becoming more responsible with credit.

3.4 Debit vs. Credit: What's the Difference and Which Should You Use?

Making financial decisions as a teen can be daunting, especially when choosing between a debit card and a credit card. Both cards look similar and swipe and tap the same way, but they function under very different principles. Understanding these differences ensures you make informed choices about managing your money effectively.

Debit cards are tied directly to your bank account. Think of them as digital keys to your checking account; when you buy something, the money is deducted straight from your bank balance. It's real-time spending of the money you already have. Credit cards, however, function more like a loan. They allow you to borrow cash up to a certain limit to pay for goods and services. The lender, usually a bank, fronts the money, and you pay it back, often with interest if not paid in full monthly.

Let's talk about the pros and cons of each. Debit cards are great for keeping your spending in check. Since they only allow you to use your own money, it's harder to overspend, making them a useful tool for budgeting. They're also generally cheaper because they don't come with high fees or interest rates unless you have an overdraft, which is when you spend more than what's in your account. However, this direct link to your money can be a double-edged sword. If your debit card information is stolen, fraudulent charges can drain your bank account quickly and recovering that money can be a hassle.

Credit cards, on the other hand, offer several advantages, especially when building a credit history. Regular, responsible credit card use can help you build good credit, making it easier and cheaper to get loans for big purchases like a car or education later. Credit cards also offer better consumer protection against fraud. If your card is used fraudulently, you're typically off the hook for those charges if you report them promptly. Credit cards often include rewards like cash back, travel points, or other benefits. However, the temptation to spend money you don't actually have is a significant downside. You can easily fall into debt if you're not careful, especially with high interest rates compounding the problem.

Choosing between debit and credit can also impact your broader financial habits. Using a debit card can reinforce the habit of spending within your means. It's a straightforward exchange—money goes out, and purchases come in. There's no worry about future bills or accruing interest. On the flip side, when used wisely, credit cards can teach you about managing debt and understanding the implications of borrowing, including the importance of interest rates and the concept of creditworthiness.

Safety features are also a key consideration. Both cards offer fraud protection, but credit cards often have more robust security features. For instance, many credit card companies monitor unusual spending patterns and quickly alert you to potential fraud, something that's especially useful when shopping online. Debit cards, while secure, can pose higher risks because they provide direct access to your funds. Having said that, many banks have improved their security measures for debit cards, implementing two-factor authentication and setting withdrawal and purchase limits to help keep your money safe. It is advisable to set up this two-factor authentication on your account.

Understanding these differences and how each card type works in line with your financial goals and habits can help you make smarter choices about which to use and when. Whether you're filling up your car's tank and would rather make an immediate payment using your debit card or booking a flight and want the protection and rewards of a credit card, knowing how each card works empowers you to take control of your financial landscape. As you grow more comfortable with financial management, you'll find that choosing between debit and credit becomes a strategic decision, not just a matter of convenience.

3.5 Protecting Yourself Against Identity Theft and Fraud

In this digital age, your personal information is like gold, and people are always trying to mine it. Anyone can be a victim of identity theft and fraud. As a teen navigating online spaces, you must know the risks and how to shield yourself. Think of the internet as a big city. It's exciting and full of opportunities, but just like in any big city, you must know how to stay safe. Identity theft involves someone stealing your personal information, such as your Social Security number or bank account details, and using it to commit fraud, like opening credit cards in your name or draining your bank accounts.

One common way this happens is through phishing attacks. These are sneaky emails or messages that look like they're from a legit company—say, your bank or a popular online store—but are actually from criminals trying to trick you into giving them your personal info. They might ask you to click on a link and log in to your account, but the link takes you to a fake site that steals your username and password. Another method is malware, malicious software that can get installed on your device without you realizing it, often through dodgy downloads or attachments. Once installed, it can spy on you, stealing passwords and account numbers as you type them.

So, how do you protect yourself? Strong, unique passwords are your first line of defense. Using a mix of letters, numbers, and symbols is advisable, and avoid obvious choices like your name or birthday. Using the same password everywhere might be tempting because it's easier to remember, but this also makes it easier for hackers. If they get your password for one account, they've got it for all your accounts. Using a password manager can help by creating and storing complex passwords for you. Two-factor authentication (2FA) adds another layer of security. Even if someone does get your password, 2FA means they also need a second code (usually sent to your phone) to get into your account, which they won't have.

Being cautious about what you share online is also key. Think before you post or fill out forms online. Do they really need to know your address or phone number? The less personal information you have out there, the less there is for thieves to find. Also, be wary of public Wi-Fi. It's super convenient to log onto the free internet in coffee shops or libraries, but these networks aren't always secure. Using your phone's data connection is safer if you're doing anything sensitive, like checking your bank account.

Now, what if, despite your best efforts, you suspect you've been a victim of fraud? First, don't panic. Contact your bank right away to report the issue and any unauthorized transactions. They can help secure your account, track the fraud, and return your money. Next, report the scam to the Federal Trade Commission (FTC) through their website, Identitytheft.gov. They can guide you through the steps, depending on what type of fraud you've experienced. They can put a fraud alert on your credit reports, which informs creditors to verify your identity using extra steps before opening any new accounts in your name.

Let's examine a real-life scenario to see why these steps are essential. Imagine a teenager, let's call her Zoe. She received an email that looked like it was from her favorite online store, asking her to update her payment details. The email had the store's logo and everything, but it was a phishing scam. Zoe entered her credit card details on the fake website, and soon after, she noticed several strange charges on her account. Because she acted quickly, contacting her bank to report the fraud and following the steps to secure her accounts, she minimized the damage. She protected her personal information from further misuse.

Staying vigilant and knowing how to protect yourself can make all the difference. In the vast digital landscape, your personal information is precious. Treat it carefully by guarding it as you would with anything valuable. Always question, verify, and remember that if something online feels off, it probably is. By taking these precautions, you can navigate the internet much more safely, keeping your digital self just as secure as your physical self.

3.6 Understanding Loans: Types, Risks, and Benefits

When you hear "loan," you might think of large amounts of money exchanged for big life events like buying a house. But loans come in all shapes and sizes, and they can be a practical tool for achieving goals at various stages of life—even during your teen years. Let's unpack the different types of loans you might encounter, understand when taking a loan makes sense, and discuss how to handle them responsibly to avoid potential pitfalls.

Types of Loans
As a teen, a few types of loans might be relevant to you.
- **Student Loans**: These are likely the first type that comes to mind. These are loans taken out to cover the costs of college tuition and other related expenses. They can be a gateway to education opportunities that might otherwise be out of reach financially.

- **Auto Loans**: Consider auto loans, especially if you're looking to buy your first car. These loans are specifically used to purchase vehicles, and they typically have terms that range from two to seven years.

- **Personal Loans**: These are a broader category that can be used for anything—from consolidating high-interest debt (not usually a teen issue) to funding a big project or purchase.

Each type of loan serves different purposes and comes with its terms and conditions. Understanding precisely what each loan offers and how it aligns with your needs is vital before you decide to take one on. Student loans have lower interest rates and deferred payment options, making them a potentially good choice for funding your education. Auto loans, meanwhile, can help you purchase a vehicle, but they often require down payments and could come with higher interest rates.

Evaluating Need and Capability

Before deciding to take out a loan, ask yourself a few questions and reflect on it: Is it truly necessary? Am I capable of handling the repayment? As a young person, your credit is fresh, and it is a lot easier to borrow. Banks and other credit organizations are happy to encourage you to take on a loan, which is debt in the long run. Ask yourself if the loan is for something essential or a want that can be postponed or saved for in other ways. It's crucial to look beyond the immediate gratification of purchasing and consider the long-term commitments involved.

Once you've determined that a loan is necessary, evaluate your capability to repay it. This involves looking at your income, if you have any, and your expected future income, especially when considering student loans. Create a mock-up budget, including your loan payments, to see if they are realistically manageable within your financial constraints. Always remember that taking on a loan is a significant responsibility. If you default on a loan, it can have severe implications, including damaging your credit score and legal repercussions.

Risks Associated with Borrowing

The risks of borrowing are largely tied to what happens if you fail to meet your repayment obligations. Defaulting on a loan can severely impact your credit score, a crucial factor in your financial identity. Having a poor credit score can impact your ability to borrow money in the future, get good rates on insurance, or even affect job opportunities. Legal repercussions can also arise, especially if you fail to repay large loans; lenders may take legal action to recover their money, which could involve reclaiming property or garnishing wages.

Benefits of Responsible Borrowing

However, when managed wisely, borrowing can be advantageous. Handling a loan can help you build a positive credit history, which will benefit future financial endeavors. You might have to start off your credit journey, by taking a credit card with a low credit limit and pay off purchases monthly to build your credit. I was once listening to a money show and a young man rang in to ask why he had worked so hard to save up for a deposit for his first apartment, but he could not get a mortgage. The difficulty was, he had no credit history, and no lender was willing to trust him with such a large sum of money without first seeing his history of repaying smaller debts. For instance, consistently making student loan payments on time can demonstrate to future lenders that you are a reliable borrower. This positive credit history can make loans for other big purchases, like homes, more accessible and cheaper. Furthermore, loans can enable you to make significant investments in your future, such as through education or acquiring a vehicle, leading to better earning opportunities.

Understanding loans, how they work, when they're helpful, and the responsibilities they entail is a fundamental aspect of personal financial literacy. As you grow and your financial goals evolve, the knowledge you gain now about managing debt will empower you to make smarter decisions, invest in your future, and achieve financial stability. Remember, a loan is not just borrowed money; it's a tool that, when used correctly, can help pave the way for a prosperous financial future.

As we close this chapter on the basics of banking and credit, remember that each financial decision you make, whether it's choosing a bank account, handling credit, or taking out a loan, contributes to the foundation of your financial independence. Next, we'll explore how to grow and protect your wealth, ensuring you manage your money and make it work for you most effectively.

Activity

If you have not opened your bank account yet, this is the opportunity to do so.

- *Find 5 banks.*

- *Enlist the help of your parents or older siblings to choose the best bank account for you.*

- *Think about the interest rates at each bank and what free or special offers the bank offers.*

- *Decide on a bank and learn about the account opening process.*

- *Open a savings account and a checking account. Remember that fees may apply to the checking account, so check whether this is the case.*

- *Decide if you want a debit card for the account, as this will give you instant access to your money. The downside, however, is that you may spend more than you want to!*

- *Deposit your allowance/income.*

Remember that this is your first step in truly understanding the world of finance, and the decision you make here can greatly impact your future finances!

MID BOOK REVIEW
Make a Difference with Your Review; Unlock the Power of Giving and Sharing.

"True happiness comes from giving and helping others."
- Oprah Winfrey

Have you ever noticed how good it feels to help someone? When we help others, we not only make their day better, but we also make our own lives richer and fuller. Now, I have a small favor to ask...

Would you be willing to help someone you've never even met, just because it's the right thing to do? Who is this person, you ask? They're a teen just like you, trying to learn how to manage their money, make smart decisions, and create a secure future. They're just starting out, and they could use a little guidance; guidance that your review of Money Skills for Teens could help provide. Our mission is to make Money Skills for Teens accessible to every teenager who needs it. Everything I do stems from that mission. And the best way for me to reach more teens is with your help. Most people do judge a book by its cover... and its reviews. So, on behalf of a teen you've never met who's eager to learn how to save, budget, and invest.

Please help that teen by leaving this book a review.

Your review doesn't cost a thing and takes less than 60 seconds, but it could change a teens' life forever. Your kind words might help one more teen understand how to save for the future. To feel that 'feel-good' feeling and really make a difference, all you must do is click the link below and leave a review. It's that simple!

https://www.amazon.co.uk/review/review-your-purchases/?asin=B0DCLBJ92S

https://www.amazon.com/review/review-your-purchases/?asin= B0DCLBJ92S

Free Bonus eBook and Workbook:

Bonus one

"Teen Cash Flow: The Quick Guide to Earning Money Online and Building Multiple Income Streams"

Bonus Two

8 Days to Financial Savvy; A Step-by-Step Workbook for Setting up Teen Personal Finance

To get these for free please email: K.emmanuel2024@yahoo.com

Coming Soon!

 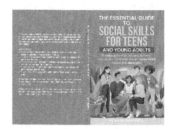

If you would like advance reader's copy of the above book, please email k.emmanuel2024@yahoo.com

See Authors Page for other books by this author.

https://www.amazon.com/stores/Kemi-Emmanuel/author/B0DCJ7RZCF?

If you're someone who enjoys helping others, you're my kind of person. I can't wait to help you achieve a financially secure future through saving, budgeting, financial planning, spending, and investing faster and easier than you ever thought possible. You're going to love the strategies we explore together in this book.

Thank you from the bottom of my heart. Now, let's get back to your journey toward financial freedom!

- Your biggest fan,

  Kemi Emmanuel

PS: Fun fact: When you help others, it makes you feel even more valuable. If you believe this book could help another teen you know, why not send it their way? Sharing is caring!

Chapter4:
Into the World of Earning

Congratulations on opening your first bank account. Are you ready to turn your passions and skills into real cash? This chapter is all about making your own money. Whether it's landing your first part-time job, setting up a side gig, or even launching a mini business, earning your own money is not only empowering; it gives you a taste of independence and a chunk of financial freedom. And let's be honest, buying things with money you've earned yourself feels great, right? But before you start imagining all the cool stuff you can buy, let's talk about how to get there, starting with landing a job.

4.1 Finding Your First Part-Time Job: Tips and Tricks

Resume Building for Teens

Creating your first resume might seem daunting, but it's an exciting opportunity to start telling your story. Your resume is like your personal highlight reel. Start by listing any formal or informal work you've done, like babysitting, lawn mowing, or even helping the family business ventures. Take advantage of volunteer work such as work in church or school projects, especially those where you held a leadership role or contributed significantly. These experiences might not seem like 'real jobs' to you. Still, they highlight how responsible you are, showing you can handle tasks and work with others.

Here's how to structure your resume:

1. **Contact Information**: Begin with your contact information at the top.

2. **Objective Statement**: Write a brief, objective statement that outlines what kind of job you're looking for and why.

3. **Education**: List your school and any relevant courses you've taken.

4. **Work Experience**: Detail your work experience, starting with the most recent.

5. **Skills**: For each entry, include your role, the place you worked, the dates you worked there, and bullet

points describing your responsibilities and achievements. If you've got skills like coding and graphic design or are proficient in a second language, add a skills section at the end.

6. **References**: you can add a reference section if you have someone such as a previous employer or manager who can put in a good word for you.

Activity
Create your 1st resume. Ask your parents or members of your family such as your siblings to assist you.

Job Search Strategies

Finding a job can be a job in itself but knowing where to look makes it easier. Start online with job platforms like Indeed, Monster, or Snagajob, which often have sections dedicated to part-time and entry-level positions.

Don't underestimate the power of your local network—let friends, family, and neighbors know you're looking for work. Sometimes, opportunities come from unexpected places. Remember to check local community boards and the websites of nearby businesses. Many small businesses don't advertise widely, so walking in and asking about openings can be a surprisingly effective strategy. It worked for my teenage daughter, who was determined to get a job after we moved into a new area. She identified the local shopping mall and walked into several shops, leaving her resume with them. She finally got a job on the day. This also worked for me as a teenager. I decided I wanted to work in a hotel at the time, and I walked into several upmarket hotels in a prominent part of town. I was offered a job on the day. So do not underestimate this strategy for finding a job. It actually works!

Interview Preparation

Landing an interview is exciting but sitting down for one can be nerve-wracking. Preparation is key. Start by researching the company. Understanding what they do and a bit about their culture shows you're interested and proactive. Practice answers to common interview questions like, "What are your strengths and weaknesses?" or "Why do you want to work here?" Try to frame your answers to highlight your skills and how they align with the job. Dress appropriately for the interview, usually, business casual is a safe bet unless it's a formal setting, then ramp it up to professional attire. Most importantly, be punctual, polite, and genuine.

Understanding Employee Rights

It is crucial to understand your rights before diving into your first job. Laws vary by location, but generally, you should be aware of your rights related to minimum wage, work hours, and workplace safety. For instance, specific labor laws prevent teens from working too late on school nights. Websites like the U.S. Department of Labor can provide information if you need clarification on the rules. Knowing your rights gives you control; it empowers you to advocate for yourself in the workplace.

Navigating the job market can be challenging, but it's also an opportunity to learn about the working world and where you fit into it. Each step builds skills you'll use throughout life, from preparing your resume to completing your interview. Why not take a deep breath, put your best foot forward, and get ready to earn money and valuable experience that will enrich your understanding of the world of work. Remember, every professional starts somewhere, and this is your beginning.

4.2 Side Hustles for Teens: Turning Passions into Pay

Imagine turning something you love doing into a way to make some extra cash. That's what a side hustle is all about! You don't always need money to start earning; sometimes, your skills and hobbies are enough. Take, for instance, learning a skill online. My daughter, at 11, began learning how to braid hair through online tutorials. With just a mannequin I provided to practice on, she honed in her skills, and by 16, she was braiding hair professionally. This didn't just fill her pockets; it expanded her skills and confidence, all without initial financial investment except for the dummy which cost me!

Identifying Marketable Skills
How do you figure out what you can offer? Start by listing things you're good at or enjoy. Are you the friend everyone comes to for help with math homework? Tutoring could be your thing. Love making bracelets or customizing your clothes? That's a craft you could turn into cash. If you're great with pets, consider dog walking or pet sitting. The key is to identify skills that not only do you enjoy but also that others might pay for. Take a moment to think about what friends or family have complimented you on or asked for your help with—that could be your golden ticket to a successful side hustle. Also think about skills you can probably learn on you tube which can bring you an income. There are loads of them!

Setting Up a Side Business

Once you pinpoint your skill, it's time to get to business. Setting up a side business can be simple. Start with a simple plan: what you'll offer, how much you'll charge, and who your customers might be. For example, if you're planning to sell handmade jewelry, consider cost-effective materials to start with, set fair prices not just for customers but that also allow you a profit, and think about where to sell such as school fairs, local markets, or online platforms like Etsy.

My older daughter started a confectionery business at just 13, selling snacks at school. With the minimal capital I provided for her initial stock, she learned firsthand how to manage money, market her products by offering little bonuses like 'buy one, get one at half price,' and even negotiate. These early lessons in entrepreneurship helped her develop skills that has made her a top-notch sales negotiator much later in her career.

Leveraging Online Platforms

The internet is a fantastic resource for reaching a wider audience. Platforms like Etsy for handmade goods, Shopify for products and services, Fiverr for freelance services such as graphic design, or even setting up a profile on social media such as "Instagram" can help you get the word out about your side hustle. These platforms handle many logistics, like payments and marketing, so you can focus on what you do best. Plus, they allow you to work from anywhere and set your own schedule, perfect for balancing school and other activities.

Time Management Tips

Speaking of balancing, managing your time is crucial when you're juggling school and a side hustle. Diving into your new business can be tempting, but prioritizing your schoolwork is vital. Block out time dedicated to your side hustle, just like you would for homework or sports practice. Be realistic about what you can handle, and don't be afraid to say no or scale back if it's affecting your schoolwork or stress levels. Remember, the goal is to enhance your life, not make it more chaotic.

Exploring the world of work is a great way to earn some extra money and a valuable opportunity to develop new skills, build confidence, and learn about the business world naturally and practically. Whether crafting, tutoring, coding, or something entirely unique, your passion can open doors to exciting opportunities. So, turn that hobby or skill into a profitable venture that adds value and joy to your life.

4.3 How to Start a Small Business as a Teen

Business Idea Generation

Kicking off your own business starts with that lightbulb moment—finding that one idea that sparks your passion and fits into a market need. Start by jotting down your interests and hobbies, then think about how they might fill a gap in the market. For example, you could create custom gaming accessories if you're an avid gamer. Or, if you love fashion, consider upcycling vintage clothes. The key is finding something you're passionate about, which will keep you motivated when the going gets tough.

To validate your idea, take a look at current market trends. Social media and online forums can provide insights into your peers' interests. Tools like Google Trends can show you what people are searching for and help you spot emerging trends. Once you have a concept, test it with friends or family or conduct a small online survey. Feedback is golden—it helps refine your idea and ensures an actual demand for your offer. Remember, a successful business solves a problem or fulfills a desire, so make sure your idea does one (or both!) of these things.

Legal and Regulatory Guidelines

Navigating the legal landscape might not be the most thrilling part of starting a business, but it's crucial. There are specific laws about minors running businesses, depending on where you live. You might need a parent or guardian to sign legal documents or help you open a bank account for your business.

Start by researching local business regulations. Your city or town hall is an excellent place to start; many places have online resources. You may need a business license, even if you are operating from home. Understanding tax obligations is also essential. The IRS website has resources to help you determine your tax liabilities as a young entrepreneur. It's a lot to take in, so consider asking a mentor or a family member with business experience to help guide you through this process. Remember, legally setting up your business protects you and builds customer credibility.

Financial Planning for Startups

Your business's financial health starts with good planning. Begin by listing your startup costs. These include materials, necessary equipment, marketing, and website hosting fees. Next, create a budget. It's important to keep track of all your income and expenses. A simple spreadsheet can help you stay organized or use essential accounting software for small businesses.

Reinvesting profits back into your business is crucial for growth. It might be tempting to spend your first earnings, but consider using them to enhance your business, like improving your website or increasing your marketing efforts. This approach helps create a sustainable business that can grow over time.

Case Studies of Successful Teen Entrepreneurs
Take inspiration from teens who have turned their entrepreneurial dreams into reality. Consider someone like Moziah Bridges, who started Mo's Bows at nine. His passion for fashion and his grandmother's teachings on sewing helped him start a business selling handcrafted bow ties. He even appeared on "Shark Tank," boosting his company into a full-blown success. There's also Mikaila Ulmer, who founded Me & the Bees Lemonade at just four years old. Starting with her family's flaxseed lemonade recipe, she expanded her business while dedicating some of her profits to saving honeybees. These stories show that with passion, a solid business plan, and the courage to take that first step, age is just a number when it comes to entrepreneurship.

Starting your own business as a teen is an exciting venture that teaches you about more than just making money. It's about creating value, learning to face challenges head-on, and understanding the market. Every step, from idea generation to financial planning, is a learning opportunity that builds a business and a future leader in you. So, ground your brilliant idea with solid research and planning and set forth confidently. Your business journey starts now!

4.4 Using Social Media to Boost Your Earnings

Let's talk about something you probably do daily scrolling through social media. But did you know your Instagram story or TikTok dance could be a goldmine? Your online presence isn't just for likes and shares; it can be a powerful tool to make real cash. Whether you aim to attract potential employers with your professional profile or want to turn your followers into customers, let's dive into how you can use social media to boost your earnings.

Building an Online Presence

Creating a professional online presence is like building your own brand. Start by choosing the right platforms. While Instagram and TikTok are great for visuals and creative content, LinkedIn is key for a more professional online profile, especially if you're eyeing job opportunities. Your profiles should represent the best version of you—think of them as your digital first impression. Ensure your content is clean, engaging, and reflects your skills and passions. For instance, if you're into photography, your Instagram could be a portfolio of your best shots. Regular updates and high-quality posts can attract not only more followers but also potential employers or clients who might be interested in your work.

Here's a pro tip: engage with your audience. Respond to comments, ask questions in your posts, and interact with other accounts. Engagement boosts your visibility and helps create a community around your brand. Also, consistency is key. Regular posts keep you on people's radar and show you're active and committed to your profile. It's not just about posting often but about posting intelligent, high-quality content that adds value and can set you apart from just another social media user to a respected online influencer or a professional worth hiring.

Social Media Marketing Basics

To turn your social media activity into a marketing tool, you need to understand the basics of digital marketing. Start by defining your target audience. Who are they? What do they like? What problems can you solve for them? Once you know who you're talking to, you should tailor content to meet their needs and interests. Use hashtags strategically to help you reach a wider audience and consider the timing of your posts to guarantee maximum visibility. For instance, posting your content during peak hours at a time when your audience is most active can significantly increase engagement rates.

Creating compelling content is at the heart of social media marketing. Whether it's informative posts, entertaining videos, or stunning visuals, your content should be something people want to see and share. Don't be afraid to show your personality—people connect with people, not just faceless brands. And remember, authenticity wins. Be genuine in your posts; your audience will appreciate and trust you more, which is crucial when monetizing your presence.

Monetizing Social Media

Now, let's get to the exciting part—making money. You can make money from your social media presence in many ways. Sponsored posts are one of the most common. Brands can pay you to promote products or services on your social media platform. This works well once you have a sizable following and a clear niche. Affiliate marketing is another route. You promote a product and get a commission for every sale through your link. This can be a great option if you have engaged followers, even if they aren't in large numbers.

Selling digital products is another avenue. If you're a graphic designer, sell your designs; if you're a musician, sell your music. You can create digital products once, and you can sell these repeatedly online, potentially earning you passive income. Platforms like Gumroad or Shopify can facilitate the selling of these products directly to your followers.

Online Safety and Privacy

While building your online presence, staying safe and protecting your personal information is crucial. Always think twice before sharing personal details that could be used against you, like your location, contact information, or personal schedule. Always use strong and unique passwords for your social media accounts and enable two-factor authentication. This provides an extra layer of security. Be cautious about scams and phishing attempts—always verify the identity of people you interact with and never share your account details.

Remember, managing your social media presence for business requires balancing openness and privacy. You can share your passions and attract opportunities without compromising your safety. As your digital footprint grows, so does your responsibility to protect it. So, whether you're just starting out or looking to enhance your existing online presence, understanding how to effectively use social media can open up numerous opportunities to boost your earnings. These tools are at your fingertips every time you log in, from creating engaging content and marketing smartly to monetizing your influence and ensuring online safety. So next time you're online, think of it as scrolling through feeds and leading you into a vast marketplace of ideas and opportunities where your contributions can add value and become tangible rewards.

4.5 Negotiating Your Allowance: Tips for Talking Money with Parents

Talking about money with your parents might be awkward, especially when negotiating your allowance. But hey, it's a perfect opportunity to show your maturity and that you are financially mature. So, how do you get started? First, consider this a professional discussion, like a business negotiation where both sides must see mutual benefits. You will need to think of what you are offering in return and don't just think they are my parents or it's my entitlement. This mindset will hinder you from learning how the world of finance works.

Preparing Your Case

Start by preparing a solid case for why you think an increase in your allowance is justified. This isn't just about saying, "I want more money." It's about demonstrating why you deserve it. Begin by assessing how you currently manage the money you receive. Are you saving a portion? Have you been responsible with the funds? Outline these points clearly. Next, think about what responsibilities you have that justify a higher allowance. Perhaps you've taken on more chores at home, or your expenses have grown because you're now involved in more extracurricular activities that require funds. Document all this because concrete examples will make your case stronger.

When you're laying out your argument, consider your parents' values and what they value. If they are big on saving, highlight how an increase in allowance could help you save more. If they appreciate responsibility, explain how managing money can help you become more responsible. This alignment between their values and your request can oftentimes tilt the scales in your favor.

Effective Communication Strategies

Choosing the right time and approach for this conversation is crucial. You want to avoid mentioning this topic when your parents are busy or stressed. Pick a time when you can have their full attention, such as a quiet evening or weekend afternoon. Approach the conversation with respect and maturity, show them you've thought this through seriously and are not just asking on a whim.

Use clear and respectful language. Instead of starting with a demand, try expressing appreciation for what your parents have already given you. Explain what you've been thinking about and how an increase could benefit your personal growth and responsibility. Be ready to negotiate, too. They might not agree to the amount you first mention, so consider what you will accept before you start the conversation.

Contributing to Household Chores

One effective way to justify a higher allowance is by offering to take on more responsibilities around the house. There may be tasks nobody likes to do, or your parents have been considering getting help from outside. Offer to take over some of these responsibilities. This shows initiative and directly links the increase in your allowance to a tangible contribution to household maintenance.

Make a list of chores you can handle and present this as part of your negotiation. This could include anything from doing laundry to managing the recycling and garbage every week. Showing them that you're ready to contribute more significantly to the household can help justify an increase in your allowance.

Setting Financial Goals Together

Finally, I suggest setting some financial goals together. This can be a powerful way to engage your parents in your financial growth and demonstrate the seriousness of your request. Discuss what you aim to achieve with your allowance: saving for college, buying educational materials, or funding a personal project like building a computer or starting a small online business.

Ask them for their input and advice on reaching these goals. This helps strengthen your case for increased allowance and turns it into a joint venture where your parents can see their direct contribution to your goals. It transforms the conversation from a simple request for more money into discussing your future and financial education.

Negotiating your allowance isn't just about getting more money each month; it's a learning experience that builds your communication and negotiation skills, teaches you about the value of money and responsibility, and deepens your relationship with your parents. So, take a deep breath, prepare your points, and confidently approach the conversation. You got this!

4.6 Financial Planning for Big Purchases: A Step-by-Step Guide

When you start thinking about making big purchases like a fancy new laptop for gaming or even your dream car, it's not just about the thrill of owning something cool. It's about setting goals, planning, saving, and making intelligent choices. Let's break down how you can approach this exciting phase of financial growth.

Goal Setting

First up, setting realistic goals for big purchases is crucial. Say you want to buy a high-end laptop. It's tempting to think, "I want that now!" However, a more practical approach starts with understanding how much it costs and setting a timeline for when you'd like to buy it. For example, if it costs $500 and you want to buy it in five months, you need to save $100 monthly to make that happen. It is important to set SMART goals; Specific, Measurable, Attainable, Realistic and Timebound. E.g $500 is specific, it is measurable as you know if you have $500 in your bank account. It is attainable, realistic and can be obtained in a certain time frame which you set according to your budget.

Start by writing down your goal and the steps needed to get there. This might include the item's cost, your current savings, if any, how much you need to save each month, and additional costs like accessories or warranties. Seeing this plan on paper or digitally makes your goal more concrete and achievable, helping you stay motivated and focused, especially when tempted to spend on other things.

Saving Strategies

Next, let's talk about effective saving strategies. A solid approach is to set aside a percentage of all income from your part-time job, allowance, or any other source. You can save 25% of every dollar you earn. Automating this process can make it easier, so why not set up a savings account that automatically transfers this percentage each time you deposit money? This way, you're consistently building your savings without thinking about it every time.

To boost your savings, look for additional income opportunities or cut back on less essential expenses. Even small savings can add up quickly, giving your budget a nice boost without feeling like you're sacrificing too much.

Research and Comparison Shopping

Doing your homework before making a big purchase can save you money and hassle. Start by researching the item you want to buy. Read reviews, watch videos, and compare different models and brands to find the best fit for your needs and budget. Look for sales, discounts, or refurbished models, which can be much cheaper than buying new.

Comparison shopping is key. Use apps or websites that compare prices across different retailers. Sometimes, waiting for seasonal sales like Black Friday or back-to-school promotions can also lead to significant savings. Remember, the goal is to get the best value for your money, so taking the time to shop around is crucial.

Plan for Unexpected Expenses

Finally, always plan for additional costs that might come up. For example, consider expenses like insurance, maintenance, and gas if you're saving for a car. For tech gadgets, think about accessories, software, or extended warranties. Setting aside a little extra for these unexpected costs ensures you won't be caught off guard and can enjoy your purchase without stress.

You can make thoughtful and successful big-ticket purchases by visualizing your goals, steadily saving, doing thorough research, and planning for extra costs. This approach gets you the items you want. It builds your financial planning and decision-making skills, setting you up for bigger financial challenges.

As we wrap up this chapter, remember that earning and managing money is just the beginning. We've explored how you can turn your skills into income, make smart money moves, and plan for those big dream purchases. Each step you take builds your confidence and knowledge, empowering you to make wise financial decisions that will benefit you for years. Next, we'll dive into how to protect and grow your money, ensuring you can enjoy the rewards of your hard work with peace of mind. Stay tuned because your financial adventure is just getting started!

Chapter5:
Investing for the Future

Welcome to the exciting world of investing! Consider this chapter your gateway to understanding how to grow your money, not just sit idle in a savings account. Imagine planting a seed today and watching it flourish over many years. That's what investing can do for your money. And the best part? You can start immediately. In fact, the earlier you begin, the better off you'll be. Let's dive into why kicking off your investment journey as a teen makes perfect sense and could be one of the most intelligent decisions you'll ever make. Remember, the sooner you start, the more you'll benefit in the long run.

5.1 Introduction to Investing: Why Start Young?

Early Advantage of Time

One of the most incredible things about starting to invest when you're young is the power of time. Time is like a secret ingredient that can turn small amounts of money into a treasure chest. It's all thanks to something known as compounding, which we'll explore more deeply later. Just know that the longer your money is invested, the more it can grow. Each year, you earn returns on both your original investment and the returns from previous years. This snowball effect can turn your modest savings from part-time jobs and birthday money into a significant sum over decades. It's like turning your pennies into dollars, then turning those dollars into more dollars, and so on.

Starting young also gives you a unique advantage in risk management. Investing has ups and downs; markets fluctuate, and investment values rise and fall. However, when you start early, you have the luxury of time to ride out any lows and take advantage of the highs. This means you can potentially afford to take on more risk (and thus, higher returns) because you have plenty of time to recover from any dips in the market.

Learning by Doing

Investing isn't just about making money; it's a fantastic way to learn about the financial markets, how different investment vehicles work, and what economic factors impact your investments. By starting young, you get hands-on experience early. You learn by doing, which is often the best way to understand complex concepts. Whether buying a few shares of stock from companies you like, investing in bonds, or starting with mutual funds, each investment teaches you something new about building wealth and managing financial risk.

Consider starting small. Many platforms allow you to invest with minimal amounts, and they can offer tools that help beginners make informed decisions. This approach minimizes risk while giving you real-world experience. Plus, making investment decisions (under the guidance of a parent or guardian) can boost your confidence in handling money and making financial decisions.

Building Financial Confidence

Speaking of confidence, regularly engaging in investment activities can significantly boost your financial confidence. Understanding investment concepts and watching your decisions play out in real time demystifies much of what seems complex or intimidating about the financial world. This newfound understanding and confidence can empower you to make more informed decisions, ask critical questions, and take greater control of your financial future.

As you become more familiar with investing, you'll recognize opportunities and risks, making you more adept at navigating the financial world. This kind of knowledge is incredibly empowering. It gives you the confidence to make financially rewarding decisions aligned with your goals.

Future Financial Freedom

Now, let's talk about the big picture—your future. Investing can be critical in achieving long-term financial goals, whether paying for college, buying a car, starting a business, or even retiring early. The money you invest now could help fund your education, and you don't have to rely on student loans or borrow capital to launch your dream startup.

Investing isn't just about building wealth; it's about creating options and opportunities for your future self. It's about personal freedom and the ability to choose based on what you want out of life, not just what you can afford. Investing wisely from a young age sets you up for financial independence, enabling you to pursue your dreams with few constraints. It's about building a life of choices, freedom, and security.

Visual Element: Chart of Compound Interest

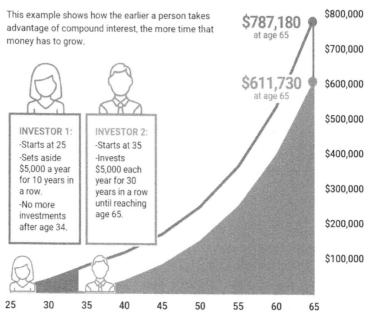

COMPOUND INTEREST:
WHO WILL EARN MORE?

This example shows how the earlier a person takes advantage of compound interest, the more time that money has to grow.

$787,180 at age 65

$611,730 at age 65

INVESTOR 1:
-Starts at 25
-Sets aside $5,000 a year for 10 years in a row.
-No more investments after age 34.

INVESTOR 2:
-Starts at 35
-Invests $5,000 each year for 30 years in a row until reaching age 65.

$800,000
$700,000
$600,000
$500,000
$400,000
$300,000
$200,000
$100,000

25 30 35 40 45 50 55 60 65

NOTES: Assumes an 8 percent interest rate, compounded annually. Balances shown are approximate.
SOURCE: Author's calculations.

FEDERAL RESERVE BANK *of* ST. LOUIS

Consider this compound interest chart to visually demonstrate the power of investing early. It shows how starting your investment journey at different ages impacts your money's growth. Notice how starting earlier results in a significantly more considerable amount by the time you reach retirement, even if you invest less money overall than starting later.

This visual is a powerful reminder of why beginning your investment journey as a teen is such an intelligent move. It illustrates theoretical concepts and real-money growth over time, underscoring the tangible benefits of early and consistent investing. So, let this motivate you to explore the world of investing, learn by doing, and build a financial foundation that will support your dreams for years to come.

Example of Compound interest
For an example of compound interest, let's assume an 8% interest rate with a retirement age 65. Interest is compounded annually.

- A 25-year-old invests $5,000 every year for 10 consecutive years. After age 34, no additional investments are made, and the money is left to grow until the investor reaches age 65.

- A 35-year-old invests $5,000 annually for 30 years, retiring at age 65.

Knowing who will have more money at 65 is no big guess.
- The individual who started investing at 25 years old and made 10 total payments of $5,000 will end up with approximately $787,180 at age 65.

- The 35-year-old who made 30 total payments of $5,000 will end up with approximately $611,730 at age 65

"How compound interest works and how to estimate it. https://www.stlouisfed.org/open-vault/2018/september/how-compound-interest-works"

UNDERSTANDING THE  **RULE OF 72**

The Rule of 72 is an easy compound interest calculation to estimate how long it will take to double your money.

72 ÷ Interest rate = Years to double money

Using the rates shown, here is about how long it would take to double an initial investment.

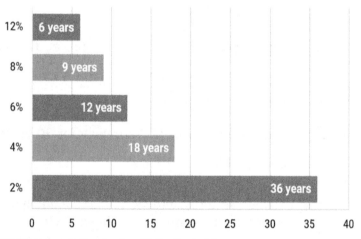

SOURCE: St. Louis Fed Econ Lowdown, "It's Your Paycheck."

FEDERAL RESERVE BANK *of* ST. LOUIS

Interactive Element: Compound Interest Calculator

Try using an online compound interest calculator to get hands-on with compound interest. These tools allow you to input different starting amounts, interest rates, and times to see how your money could grow under various scenarios. You can add regular monthly contributions alongside your initial investment to see how quickly your money grows. This interactive experience makes the concept of compound interest more tangible. It encourages you to play around with different variables to understand the potential long-term impact of various saving and investment strategies.

As we progress in this chapter, keep these foundational concepts in mind. They are abstract ideas and practical tools that can shape your financial future. Investing is more than just a way to make money, it's a way to build a life full of choices, freedom, and security. Let's explore how you can make the most of your investments and capitalize on the early start you're getting today.

5.2 Understanding Stocks, Bonds, and Mutual Funds

Diving into the world of investments, think of stocks, bonds, and mutual funds as different flavors of ice cream. Each has its unique taste and, depending on your preference, serves a distinct purpose in your financial diet.

Stocks

Let's start with stocks. When you own stock, it is owning a piece of a company. Imagine if your favorite sneaker brand was a pie, and you get a slice of that pie by buying stocks. You become a part-owner of that company. If the company does well, your slice of the pie could become more valuable, and you might receive dividends, which are like little rewards for putting your faith in the company. However, if the company does not do so well, the value of your slice can stay the same or sometimes decrease, but if you keep going, you can reap a great harvest in the long run. Stocks are exciting because they offer high potential returns. However, they also come with a higher risk because their value can change quickly based on how the company is doing and how the market feels about it.

Bonds
Now, let's talk about bonds. Imagine lending money to your friend who promises to pay you back with a little extra after some time. That's essentially what a bond is. Governments or companies issue bonds to raise money, promising to pay back the bond's face value on a specific date, plus regular interest payments along the way. These are generally considered safer than stocks because you know exactly how much you will get back if you hold the bond until its maturity date unless the issuer runs into financial trouble.

Mutual Funds

Mutual funds are like a big mixed bag of candies, where you get a little bit of everything. When you invest in mutual funds, you're pooling your money with other investors, and a professional manager is using this pool to buy a diversified mix of stocks, bonds, or other securities. This diversity helps spread the risk because even if one investment drops in value, others in the fund might be doing well. It's a way to get broad exposure to the markets without picking individual stocks or bonds yourself, and it can be a safer, more stable way to invest compared to owning individual stocks.

Visual Aid: Pie Chart of Investment Types

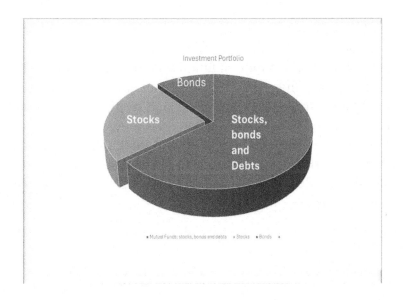

Imagine a pie chart split into three segments representing stocks, bonds, and mutual funds. Each segment is a different size, reflecting how much of your total investment portfolio they represent. This visual can help you understand the concept of diversification, showing how you can spread your investments across different types to manage risk effectively. For instance, if the stock segment is too large and the market dips, your portfolio could take a big hit. But if you have a well-balanced mix, the other segments can help stabilize your overall portfolio.

Diversification is vital in investing. It's like not putting all your eggs in one basket. If one investment fails, you have others that can perform well and balance out any losses. Mutual funds are beneficial for diversification because they inherently invest in a wide range of assets, which helps reduce significant losses.

To bring these concepts to life, let's consider a case study of a teen investor, James. James started investing a small sum of money in a mutual fund containing a mix of stocks and bonds. James watches as the value of the mutual fund fluctuates, sometimes going up and sometimes dipping down. James receives regular statements, seeing how different investments within the fund contribute to its overall performance. This real-world experience gives James an idea of how diversification can help manage investment risk.

By exploring and understanding these fundamental investment types, you're better equipped to make informed decisions about where to put your money. Whether you're drawn to the potential high returns of stocks, the relative safety of bonds, or the diversified approach of mutual funds, each type has a role in building a balanced investment portfolio. As you grow more familiar with these concepts, you'll gain the confidence to expand your investment activities and continue building a robust financial foundation for your future.

5.3 Using Apps to Start Investing with Small Amounts

Imagine turning your pocket change into a growing investment portfolio. It almost seems magical, right? Thanks to the rise of app-based investment tools, this isn't just a fantasy. These apps are designed to make the investment process super accessible and user-friendly, especially for beginners like you who might not have a lot of cash to start with. Let's walk through some of the best apps that enable you to invest only a few dollars and discuss how to pick the right one for your needs.

Apps like Acorns, Stash, and Robinhood have revolutionized how we think about investing. They break down traditional barriers to entry, such as high initial investments and complex trading platforms. Acorns, for example, uses a clever 'round-up' feature, which rounds up your daily purchases to the nearest dollar, automatically investing the difference into a diversified portfolio. So, if you buy a coffee for $3.75, Acorns rounds it up to $4 and invests the $0.25 difference. It's a painless and almost invisible way to build your savings. "Stash" offers a similar micro-investment model with added educational resources to help you learn as you grow your money. Then there's Robinhood, known for its zero-commission fee structure, which allows you to trade stocks, ETFs, and even cryptocurrencies without paying a brokerage fee on each transaction.

When choosing an investment app, consider the most essential features. User-friendliness is critical—you want an app that makes it easy to set up and manage your investments without needing a finance degree. Look for intuitive interfaces and clear, simple instructions. Educational resources are also crucial, especially if you're new to investing. Apps offering tutorials, guides, or webinars can help you build your knowledge and confidence. Finally, always consider the fees. While many apps promote low or no commissions, other costs might be associated with managing your account or withdrawing funds. Always read the fine print to understand what you might be charged.

5.4 Online Investing, Safety and Security

Now, let's discuss a critical aspect of online investing: security. Investing apps handle your money and personal information, so ensuring they do so securely is non-negotiable. First, check that any app you use employs robust security measures, such as encryption, which protects your data from hackers by making it unreadable without a specific key. Two-factor authentication (2FA) adds additional security, requiring a second form of identification to access your account, typically via a code sent to your phone.

Be cautious with your personal information. Keep your login details private from everyone. Be wary of phishing attempts—emails or messages that trick you into giving away personal information. Always access your investment app directly rather than clicking on links in emails or texts, which could lead you to fraudulent sites.
Investing can feel daunting, but remember, every expert investor was once a beginner. By using these apps, you're taking your first steps into a larger world of financial independence and growth. With each investment, you gain more knowledge and confidence. Keep learning, invest, and watch your initial small sums blossom into a more secure financial future.

Activity

Starting Your Investment Journey

Ready to start your investment journey? Here's a step-by-step guide to getting started with an investment app:

1. **Choose Your App**: Based on the features discussed, pick an app that suits your investment style and needs. Download it from a reliable source such as the App Store or Google Play to avoid counterfeit applications.

2. **Set Up Your Account**: Follow the app's setup process, which will typically involve linking your bank account and providing some basic personal information. Remember, reputable apps will have robust security measures to protect this data.

3. **Understand the Interface**: Spend some time exploring the app. Look at the different menus and options. Understanding how to use the app will make your investment process smoother and more enjoyable.

4. **Make Your First Investment**: Start small. Many apps allow you to invest with as little as $5. Choose a low-risk option initially, allowing you to observe how investing works without exposing you to significant risk.

5.5 Risks and Rewards: A Balanced View of Teen Investing

Investing might sound like an exciting way to turn your savings into serious cash, but it's more than just watching your money grow. It is essential to understand the risks involved and how to manage them. Think of it like learning to skateboard. It's thrilling and rewarding, but you need to know how to balance and when to brake to avoid a few scrapes. In the financial world, these scrapes can be losses that affect your initial investment. Let's break down the risks and how you can smartly manage them to maintain a healthy investment portfolio.

First up, there's market risk, which is just a fancy term for the ups and downs that happen in the market daily. These can be caused by factors such as economic changes, political events, or even public sentiment. It's like the weather; it can change quickly and sometimes unpredictably, affecting everything in its path. Then, there's credit risk, which comes into play when you invest in bonds or other types of debt. It's the risk that the company or government you've lent money to might be unable to pay you back. Imagine lending your skateboard to a friend who sometimes forgets to return things; there's always a chance you might not get it back.

Interest rate risk is another important one, especially when dealing with bonds. It's all about changes in the interest rate environment. If interest rates go up after you've bought a bond, the value of your bond might go down, and vice versa. It's like when you plan a day at the park, suddenly it starts raining, dampening your plans.

Navigating these risks might seem daunting, but you can manage them effectively with the right strategies. Asset allocation is a great start. It's about spreading your investments across different types of assets like stocks, bonds, and cash. Think of it as not putting all your eggs in one basket. If one basket falls, you still have the others. Diversification goes hand in hand with this. Investing in various sectors and instruments reduces the risk of a single event impacting your entire portfolio. It's like playing different sports throughout the year; if you get injured in one, you can still enjoy others.

Setting stop-loss orders can also be wise, especially for individual stock investments. You set up this instruction with your brokerage to sell a stock if it drops to a specific price, helping you avoid more considerable losses if the market dips suddenly. Picture this as wearing a helmet while skateboarding; if you fall, it helps prevent serious injuries.

Now, let's talk about the rewards because that's what makes investing exciting. However, setting realistic expectations is vital. It's easy to hear stories of stocks that skyrocket overnight and dream of significant returns, but the reality is often less dramatic. Investment returns can vary widely, and they're influenced by how much risk you're willing to take on. Generally, higher risks can lead to higher rewards and potential losses. Finding a comfortable balance that works in tandem with your financial goals is essential. Always remember, the higher the risk, the higher the rewards.

Investing is also a psychological journey. It can be thrilling to see your investments grow, but losses can be challenging to handle, especially if they're significant. That's why understanding the emotional side of investing is crucial. It's normal to feel a rush when you make a sound investment choice, but it's essential to stay grounded and not let emotions drive your decisions. Similarly, experiencing a loss can be disheartening, but it's part of the investing landscape. The key is to learn from these experiences. Do not make hasty decisions based on short-term market movements.

In your investment adventure, remember that knowledge is your best tool. The more you understand the risks and rewards, the better equipped you'll be to make decisions that excite you and move you toward your long-term personal financial goals. So keep learning, questioning, and balancing risk with potential rewards. You will thank yourself in future for the wise decisions you make today.

5.6 Setting Long-Term Investment Goals

Let's talk about setting goals. Not just any goals but long-term investment goals that can shape your future and pave the way to personal financial independence. Think of goal setting as mapping out a road trip to your favorite destination. You need a clear route (your plan), checkpoints along the way (short-term goals), and, most importantly, a destination (your long-term goal). To make this journey successful, you'll need to employ a strategy known as SMART goal setting as previously illustrated. Each element ensures that your goals aren't just wishes but actionable paths that lead to actual results.

Let's break it down with a real-life scenario. For instance, at age 16, you dream of starting your own tech company by age 20. An example of a SMART goal could be: "Save $5,000 for initial business expenses by the time I'm 20 by saving $100 from my part-time job every month". It's specific and measurable—$5,000. It's achievable if you stick to saving $100 each month. It's relevant to your entrepreneurial aspirations and time-bound—with a deadline by age 20. This framework gives clarity and focus and helps you measure progress and stay motivated.

Now, envision a few common long-term investment goals for teens like you. Funding higher education might be one. Instead of taking on hefty student loans, imagine investing in a college savings plan early. Another goal could be buying your first car. Rather than relying on high-interest financing options, you could start a dedicated savings fund that grows over time. Or you may be aiming to launch your startup like many young visionaries. Setting aside investment capital now could be the key to realizing your business idea. Setting each of these as SMART goals helps you to focus on achieving them by the time you set.

Regularly reviewing and adjusting these goals is crucial. Life is full of changes, financial situations shift, new opportunities arise, and sometimes, challenges pop up. Maybe the job market shifts, impacting how much you can save each month, or perhaps tuition fees increase. Checking in on your goals regularly, like every six months or annually, allows you to recalibrate your plan based on your current circumstances and financial performance. This might mean tweaking your monthly savings amount or adjusting your timeline.

Consistency is your best friend when it comes to investing. It's about making regular contributions to your investments, continually educating yourself about financial opportunities and pitfalls, and staying committed even when the market gets rocky. Think of your investment as a garden. To thrive, it needs regular care—watering, weeding, and occasional pruning. Similarly, your investment portfolio needs regular reviews and adjustments to align with your long-term goals.

Investing isn't just about putting money away. It's a proactive strategy for building the future you envision. By setting SMART goals, regularly adjusting your plan, and staying consistent in your efforts, you're not just saving money but paving a path to financial freedom and security. So, dream big, plan smart, and invest consistently. Your future self will thank you for the foresight and dedication you showed today.

As this chapter concludes, remember that investing is more than just accumulating wealth. It's about strategically planning for a prosperous future and taking actionable steps to realize your dreams. Whether funding your education, buying your first car, or starting a business, the principles of SMART goal setting, regular monitoring, and consistency in action are your tools for success. In the next chapter, we'll delve deeper into navigating the complexities of credit and loans, ensuring you're equipped to make informed decisions about borrowing and managing debt. Stay tuned and keep those investment goals in sight!

Chapter6:
Navigating Debt and Credit

I magine you're at your favorite store, eyeing a brand-new computer or the latest smartphone. It's just a credit card swipe away from being yours. Tempting, right? But here's the twist—every financial decision you make, including this one, can either set you up for success or hold you back. That's why understanding the difference between good and bad debt is crucial. It's not about restricting your choices but about empowering you to make decisions that benefit you in the long run, just like knowing which foods fuel your body best or which study habits get straight A's. This knowledge puts you in the driver's seat of your financial future, giving you the power to make informed decisions.

6.1 Good Debt vs. Bad

Define Good Debt and Bad Debt

Let's break it down. Good debt is like investing in your future. Taking on financial obligations can help you grow and gain more value over time. For example, student loans are considered good debt because they are an investment in your education. This can create better job opportunities and higher earning potential. This isn't just a purchase; it's a tool that enhances your learning and productivity. The long-term benefits of good debt can be a source of optimism about your financial future.

On the flip side, bad debt is the kind that doesn't bring you any return and can often cost you more than the borrowed amount due to high interest rates. Credit card debt from buying things like trendy clothes or the latest gadgets can be considered bad debt. These items don't increase in value, and if you can't pay off the balance right away, you'll be hit with interest charges that make the original purchase price balloon.

Examples That Resonate

Imagine buying that trendy $200 jacket with your credit card. Suppose you only make the minimum monthly payment, the smallest amount you must pay each month to keep your account in good standing, with an interest rate of 20%. The interest rate is the cost of borrowing money, usually expressed as a percentage of the borrowed total. In this case, it means that for every $ 100 you borrow, you have to pay an extra $ 20 in interest. That jacket can eventually cost you much more than $200, taking a long time to pay off.

Now, let's consider a different scenario. You use a student loan to fund a summer coding boot camp. This education could boost your skills, making you more marketable for tech-related jobs or internships. The initial debt has the potential to enhance your career options and income, which can pay off the loan and then some.

Long-term Impact

The effects of good and bad debt extend far into your future. Good debt management helps you build a strong credit history, which is crucial for future financial actions like renting an apartment or buying a car. A strong credit history makes getting approved for loans and credit cards with better terms easier. It can affect your ability to get a job or rent a home, as credit checks are often carried out. It can open doors to opportunities that increase your earning power. Bad debt, however, can drag down your credit score, limit your financial opportunities, and create a cycle of debt that's tough to escape. It's like being stuck in quicksand, where the deeper you sink, the more you struggle to escape the financial hole.

Decision-Making Tips

So, how do you decide when to take on debt? Always ask yourself a few key questions: Will this debt help me grow financially? Can I manage the monthly payments without stressing my budget? What's the interest rate, and how long will I pay this off? Always aim to keep your future self in mind. Opt for debt that brings value beyond the immediate gratification of a purchase, and always have a clear repayment plan.

Imagine you're planning your budget with an eye toward the future, balancing today's wants with tomorrow's needs. By understanding the types of debt and their impacts, you equip yourself with the knowledge to navigate financial decisions wisely, ensuring each step you take is toward economic stability and success. Think of it as setting up dominoes; each one you place carefully ensures a smooth, successful cascade, building up to your ultimate financial goals.

6.2 Strategies to Avoid Debt Traps

Navigating your financial landscape as a teen can sometimes feel like avoiding traps in a dense jungle. Knowing where these traps lie and how to sidestep them is crucial, especially regarding debt. Let's discuss some common traps, like payday loans and high-interest credit cards, and then walk through how a bit of smart budgeting and savvy spending can keep you safe.

It might seem like a quick fix to take on Payday loans when you need cash fast, but they're notorious for their exorbitant interest rates and fees. They can quickly become a debt spiral where you borrow more to repay the initial loan. High-interest credit cards are another pitfall. They might tempt you with offers of immediate credit. Still, the high interest can compound quickly, making it difficult to pay off the balance. Recognizing these traps is the first step. If an offer seems too good to be true, like being promised easy money without a detailed check of your financial situation, it's a red flag.

Budgeting

Budgeting is your best tool to keep out of debt. The best way to do this is to track all your income and expenses. Seeing what you are spending each month is eye-opening and can help you adjust your spending before it turns into debt. For example, if you're spending a lot on eating out, consider setting a monthly limit or cooking more meals at home. When planning significant purchases or handling emergencies, having a budget can help you save for these expenses ahead of time instead of relying on credit. Set aside a small emergency fund that you can tap into instead of using credit cards. This fund doesn't have to be huge; starting with a goal of $100 and adding to it gradually can make a big difference.

Smart Spending Habits

Developing smart spending habits is another crucial strategy. Always compare prices before purchasing and look for discounts or coupons to lower costs. Resist impulse buys by giving yourself a 24-hour "cooling-off" period before purchasing anything over a set amount— say, $50. This gives you time to consider whether you need the item or if the money could be better used elsewhere. Remembering and understanding the difference between needs and wants can help you prioritize spending. While wants are things that are nice to have, they are not necessary. When you decide to spend on a want, plan for it and ensure it fits within your budget.

When borrowing makes sense, such as taking out a student loan for college, ensure you understand all the loan terms. This includes knowing the interest rate, repayment schedule, and any fees associated with the loan. Shop around to ensure you get the best deal and read all the fine print. Ask questions like: Can the interest rate change? What happens if I miss a payment? Knowing the answers can help you borrow safely and avoid unpleasant surprises. This level of understanding can make you feel prepared and knowledgeable about your financial decisions.

By staying alert to debt traps, using a budget to guide your spending, and developing habits that maximize your savings, you're not just avoiding debt but also building a solid foundation for your financial future. Remember these strategies as you handle money, and you'll confidently navigate the financial jungle. Remember, every intelligent financial decision you make today sets the stage for your tomorrow.

6.3 How to Build and Maintain a Healthy Credit Score

Let's talk about your credit score—it's like a report card for your finances. Just as your grades reflect how well you're doing in school, your credit score shows how well you manage your money, especially when it comes to borrowing and paying it back. Understanding what affects this score, how to keep it healthy, and why it matters can prepare you for financial success beyond your teen years.

Factors Influencing Credit Score

Credit scores can feel mysterious as they are determined by complex algorithms. Still, it's actually based on a few apparent factors. First up is your payment history. This is a record of how consistently you pay your bills on time. Much of your credit score is based on whether you pay back what you owe. Next is credit utilization; this is a fancy way of asking how much available credit you're using. It's a good rule to keep this under 30%. For instance, with a credit card limit of $1,000, ensure you carry at most $300 as a balance. Then there's the length of your credit history. The longer you've been using credit responsibly, the better it is for your score. Being a teen can be challenging since you're likely just starting out. However, even being an authorized user on a parent's credit card can start to build this history.

Healthy Credit Habits

Building and maintaining a healthy credit score doesn't have to be a chore. Think of it as part of your daily routine, like brushing your teeth. Always aim to pay your bills on time. Set reminders on your phone or use automatic payments if that helps. Keeping a low credit card balance is another healthy habit. It shows that you're relying on more than just credit for all your needs, which lenders like to see. And here's a pro tip: only apply for new credit when necessary. Each time you apply for credit, your score can be temporarily decreased. So, applying for several credit cards or loans in a short period can make lenders think you're in financial trouble.

Monitoring Credit

Regularly checking your credit score, much like monitoring your social media, is a good habit. You can get a free credit report from each of the three major credit reporting agencies: Equifax, Experian, and TransUnion—once a year at AnnualCreditReport.com. This won't give you your credit score. Still, it will show you the information contributing to your score, like your credit accounts, debts, and payment history. Reviewing this report can help you catch mistakes or spot signs of identity theft early. If anything looks wrong, you can dispute it with the credit agency. It's like proofreading your essay—you want to make sure everything is accurate before it affects your grade.

Role of Credit in Personal Finance: Understanding why a good credit score matters can motivate you to keep your score intact. A solid credit score can make life's significant steps more accessible and less expensive. For example, if you buy a car on credit, lenders often check your credit score to decide if they'll give you a loan and at what interest rate. A better score can mean a lower interest rate, which saves you money. It's similar to renting an apartment; landlords might check your credit score to see if you'll pay your rent on time. Even some employers check credit scores as part of the hiring process. It's seen as a sign of responsibility and reliability. So, while it might seem like just a number, your credit score says a lot about you and can affect several aspects of your life.

Building a healthy credit score is like planting a seed for your financial future. It requires care, consistency, and sometimes a bit of patience. But the rewards, easier loan access, lower interest rates, and more financial opportunities are worth the effort. Remember these tips as you start managing your credit, and you'll be on your way to a financially healthy future.

6.4 Understanding Student Loans: A Guide for Future College Students

So, you're considering college, which means you're also considering how to pay for it. Let's dive into student loans, which can be a lifeline for funding your education and a big financial commitment. It is crucial to understand the types of student loans, how to apply for them, and strategies for managing them responsibly. It's like learning the rules of a new game where the stakes are your financial future.

Types of Student Loans
There are two main types of student loans: federal and private. Federal student loans are government-backed loans that offer flexible repayment options that are flexible and lower interest rates. They don't require a credit check (except for PLUS loans), which is excellent because many students still need to build significant credit histories. Private lenders, Banks, and credit unions offer private loans, and their terms vary widely. They often depend on your credit score to determine eligibility and interest rates, which means they can sometimes be more expensive than federal loans.

Understanding these differences is critical. Federal loans, on the one hand, offer income-driven repayment plans, which can adjust your monthly pay based on your income. This isn't typically available with private loans. Also, federal loans have deferment and forbearance, which allows you to stop payments temporarily if you're going through tough financial times again, something less acceptable with private loans.

Applying for Student Loans

Applying for student loans might seem daunting, but it's like filling out any other important application, taking it step by step makes it manageable. Initially, fill out the Free Application for Federal Student Aid (FAFSA), which is your gateway to federal loans. This form assesses your financial need and determines what kind of aid package you're eligible for, including grants (which don't need to be repaid!) and loans.

When looking at private loans, it's crucial to shop around. Check out different lenders to compare interest rates and repayment terms. Always consider the Annual Percentage Rate (APR), which includes interest rates and fees. This will give you a clearer picture of the total cost of the loan. Read the fine print and ask questions: Are there origination fees? What's the policy on late payments? Can you see yourself comfortably dealing with this lender throughout the loan?

Repayment Strategies

Once college is done, repayment kicks in, and having a strategy is crucial. You might opt for a standard repayment plan with fixed payments for federal loans, ensuring the loan is paid off within 10 years. Alternatively, income-driven plans adjust your monthly payments based on your income, which can be a relief when starting your career.

One wise strategy is to start paying off the interest while you're still in school if you can manage it. This prevents the interest from being added to your principal amount (capitalization), which can significantly increase the total amount you'll end up paying. If you find yourself in an excellent financial spot at any point, consider making more than your minimum payment each month. This accelerates your payoff timeline and reduces the total interest you pay.

Impact of Student Debt

Student debt can feel like a heavy backpack you carry around post-graduation. It can affect your ability to take risks like starting a business, making saving for other big goals like buying a house more challenging. However, proper debt management can help build your credit score, provided you make timely payments. This is crucial for your future financial dealings.

Taking on student loans is a significant decision and should fit into your broader financial picture. Consider your career path and potential earnings. Jobs in some sectors may qualify for loan forgiveness programs, which can alleviate some burdens. Always stay informed about new laws or changes in student loan regulations, as these could affect your repayment strategies.

Navigating the world of student loans with a clear understanding and a solid plan can prevent them from becoming a financial burden. Think of them as an investment in your future that needs careful and informed management. Equip yourself with the correct information and tools, and you'll be able to handle this responsibility.

6.5 Credit Card Smarts: What Teens Need to Know Before Applying

Stepping into the world of credit cards can be like unlocking a new level in a game, where new challenges and opportunities suddenly open up. It's thrilling, sure, but also something you want to navigate with a clear head and as much info as possible. Let's break down how to choose the right credit card, understand the terms that come with it, and use it to benefit you, setting you up for a solid financial future.

Choosing the Right Credit Teammate
Choosing a credit card is like picking a teammate in a sports game. You want someone reliable who's got your back. Start by looking at the fees. Some cards will charge an annual fee just for using them. Can you justify this fee with its benefits, or would a no-fee card make more sense? Next up, interest rates. This is the cost of borrowing on the card if you don't pay it off each month. Look for a card with a competitive interest rate, but remember, the goal is to pay off your balance in full, so you won't have to worry about this too much.

Then, consider the rewards or benefits. Some cards offer cashback on purchases, points for travel, or other perks like discounts at stores or freebies. Think about what benefits align with your spending habits or interests. For example, if you love shopping online, a card that offers extra points or cashback for online purchases could be a good match. Always compare a few cards to see which provides the best combination of low fees, interest rates, and valuable rewards.

Decoding Credit Card Terms
Credit card terms sometimes feel like a foreign language. APR, or Annual Percentage Rate, is one you'll see a lot. It represents the yearly cost of borrowing money on the card, including interest and fees, shown as a percentage. Another key term is the minimum payment, which is the smallest amount to be paid each month to avoid penalties. It's usually a small percentage of your total balance. Understanding these terms helps you manage your card more effectively and avoid surprises when your statement comes.

Another critical term is the grace period, the time between the end of your billing cycle and your next due payment date. During this period, interest is not charged on new purchases if you pay off the previous balance by the due date. If used wisely, this can be a great way to manage cash flow.

Responsible Use of Credit Cards

Here are some best practices to keep you on the right track. One of the simplest but most effective strategies is to always aim to make not just the minimum payment but possibly the total balance on your credit card. This helps you avoid mounting interest and keeps your debt manageable. Also, use your credit card for planned purchases rather than impulsive spending. Before you buy anything, ask yourself if it's something you had planned to buy anyway and if it fits within your budget. This helps prevent the common pitfalls of buying now and stressing about how to pay later.

Another smart habit is using your credit card for small, regular purchases you know you can immediately pay off, such as your monthly streaming service subscription. This strategy helps build a good credit history while keeping your balance low.

6.6 Handling Credit Challenges: Real Teen Scenarios and Solutions

Imagine you're in a situation where, despite your best efforts, you face a maxed-out credit card or missed a payment or two. These scenarios are more common than you think and don't have to spell disaster. Here's how to tackle these challenges head-on and keep your financial health intact.

Let's start with the scenario where you've maxed out your credit card. This can suddenly happen. If you need to keep a close eye on your spending or if an emergency forces you to exceed your limit. The first step is not to panic. Review your credit card statement to understand how you reached your limit—identifying the cause can help you plan your next moves.

The next step is to create a payment plan. Prioritize this debt because maxed-out cards can significantly affect your credit score. Consider ways to reduce your spending in other areas or, if possible, increase your income through extra jobs or selling items you no longer need. Communicating with your credit card issuer is also key. Sometimes, if you explain your situation, they might offer solutions like a temporary interest rate reduction or a payment plan that fits better with your current financial situation.

Now, let's tackle the scenario of missing a payment. This slip-up can happen to anyone, but addressing it is crucial to prevent damage to your credit score. First, pay as soon as possible, the sooner, the better. Late payments can usually be reported to credit bureaus once 30 days past due, so acting fast can prevent the issue from escalating. Next, reach out to your creditor. Explain why the payment was missed and assure them of your intention to keep up with future payments. Many creditors appreciate honesty and might be willing to waive the late fee or not report the lapse if it's a first-time occurrence. It can sometimes help to automatically set up minimum monthly payments for the amount due each month to prevent future slips. This way, you'll never miss a payment deadline.

Preventative measures are your best defense against common credit challenges. A solid starting point is to maintain a budget that tracks all your expenses and ensures you live within your means. Regular checks on your bank and credit card statements can help you catch issues before they become more significant problems. Additionally, an emergency fund can be a lifesaver. Start small and aim to save enough to cover at least one month of living expenses. This fund can cover unexpected costs without relying on credit cards, keeping your credit utilization low and manageable.

For those times when you need guidance, remember that resources are available. Websites like the National Foundation for Credit Counseling (NFCC) offer tools and advice on managing credit and debt. They can connect you with accredited financial advisors who specialize in helping people navigate their credit challenges. These resources can give you the knowledge and support to manage your finances effectively.

Navigating credit challenges successfully always requires a mix of proactive strategies, good habits, and proper support. By understanding how to manage these situations, you can maintain your financial health and build a solid financial foundation for your future. Remember, facing financial challenges isn't about enduring setbacks; it's about growing your ability to handle and overcome them, making you more financially resilient.

As this chapter wraps up, remember that the world of credit isn't just about borrowing money, it's about using financial tools to build and enhance your life. Next, we'll explore advanced financial planning techniques that will take your newfound knowledge and put it into action, preparing you for bigger financial adventures in the future. Keep these lessons in mind, and you'll be well on your way to mastering not just credit but your broader financial journey.

Chapter7:
Advanced Personal Finance Planning

L et us paint a picture: every time you make a purchase, a tiny portion of your payment goes on a journey through various government projects—from the roads you ride to the schools you attend. This is just one of the many roles' taxes play in our everyday lives. In this chapter, we'll untangle the often-confusing world of taxes to show you why they matter and how mastering this aspect of finance can give you a leg-up in managing your future earnings and savings effectively. It's not just about paying what's due—understanding taxes can lead to substantial savings. It can influence your personal financial decisions in powerful ways.

7.1 Basics of Taxes: What Teens Need to Know

Understanding the Tax System

Let's start with the basics: what exactly is a tax? Simply put, taxes are mandatory contributions levied by governments on workers' income and business profits. They are sometimes added to the cost of goods, services, and transactions. Why do we pay taxes? Well, they fund public services and infrastructure, like education, transportation, and healthcare, which play a significant role in shaping the quality of life in society. Understanding this connection can make you feel more connected to your community and the services you benefit from as a teen.

In the United States, the tax system operates at three levels: federal, state, and local. The Internal Revenue Service (IRS) manages federal taxes. They are used for national defense, social security, and federal welfare programs. For instance, your federal taxes might go towards funding the military or providing social security benefits to retirees. These taxes vary significantly between states and depend on where you live. State taxes fund state services like public safety and local education. For example, your state taxes might go towards funding your local school or police department. Local taxes, collected by counties or cities, often fund community projects such as libraries, parks, and local road maintenance. Understanding these levels helps you see where your contributions go and why they're necessary.

Types of Taxes

Now, let's dive into the different types of taxes you might encounter. The most common is income tax, which is taken directly from your earnings. Some of your income will typically go to income taxes, whether working a part-time job or running a small business. Sales tax on the other hand, is something you pay when you buy products or services. Notice how the price at the register is often higher than the sticker price? That's sales tax in action. Then there's property tax, which might not affect you directly now, but it's something your family pays if they own property. Understanding these taxes helps you better manage your spending and prepares you for future financial responsibilities.

Filing a Tax Return

One of the fundamental rites of passage into financial adulthood is filing your first tax return. It can sound daunting, but it's basically the process of telling the government how much money you made, how much tax you've already paid, and how much you should have paid. If you paid more than necessary, you might get a refund. The key here is accuracy and timeliness. You typically need to file your tax return by a specific date each year (usually April 15th), and it's crucial to be accurate to avoid penalties or audits.

For most teens, if they have a job, their employer will send them a form called a W-2, which shows how much they have earned and how much tax was withheld. You use this form to fill out your tax return. Several online platforms can guide you through filing the form; some are free if you meet specific criteria. Learning to do this is not just a necessity; it's a valuable skill that boosts your financial literacy.

Tax Deductions and Credits

Here's some good news: you can reduce how much tax you owe if you qualify for deductions and credits. Tax deductions lower your taxable income. For instance, if you earn money from a summer job and spend some of your earnings on school supplies, those expenses might qualify as deductions. Tax credits are even more exciting because they reduce your tax bill dollar-for-dollar. There are credits for educational expenses, for example, which can be helpful if you're attending college.

Understanding these can save you and your family a lot of money, making learning about them worth your time. Always keep receipts and track expenses that could qualify for these benefits. As you grow older and your financial situation becomes more complex, you will need to know how to manage any deductions and credit, as this can affect your financial health.

By grasping the fundamentals of the tax system, you are setting yourself up not just to fulfill a civic duty but to strategically enhance your finances. Taxes might seem like a small piece of the puzzle now, but as you earn more and make bigger financial decisions, what you know about taxes can mean the difference between just getting by and getting ahead. So, take this knowledge and run with it—your future self will thank you.

7.2 Insurance 101 for Teens: Types and Why It Matters

Let's talk about one of those grown-up concepts that seems distant until it suddenly is not i.e., insurance. You might hear adults discussing it all the time, often with a bit of a groan. But here's the deal: insurance is a crucial safety net as you become more independent. Think of it as a strategy game where you're managing risks. Whether it's a fender bender in your car, a broken phone, or even something as simple as losing your laptop, insurance cushions the financial blow these mishaps can bring. Understanding this can save you from headaches and sudden expenses as you navigate your teen years and beyond.

Purpose of Insurance

So, why is insurance such a big deal? At its core, insurance is about protection. It's a way to financially protect yourself from the unexpected events that life throws at you. When you buy an insurance policy, you're making a deal with an insurance company. You agree to regularly pay a certain amount, known as a premium. In return, they decide to cover the costs if certain things go wrong, like if you get into a car accident or if your apartment gets burglarized. If you didn't have insurance, you would have to pay for these costs out of your own pocket, which could be financially devastating. It's not just about covering losses; it's about giving you peace of mind. For a relatively small amount of money, you're buying yourself a promise that if the worst happens, you won't have to face it alone financially.

Common Types of Insurance

Several types of insurance might be relevant to you as a teen. Health insurance is a big one. It covers medical expenses, which can be astronomical if you have an illness or injury. If you drive, auto insurance is mandatory in most places, and it covers damages from accidents. If you're living in a dorm or renting your first place, renters' insurance can protect your belongings in case of theft or damage. Each type of insurance has specific rules about what's covered and what's not. Still, the main idea is the same: to help you manage the cost of unexpected problems.

How Insurance Works

Let's break down how these policies work. The premium is the amount you pay to keep your insurance active. It's like a subscription fee. Then there's the deductible, which you agree to pay out of pocket before the insurance covers the rest. For example, suppose you have a $500 deductible on your car insurance, and you get into an accident that causes $2000 worth of damage. In that case, you pay the first $500, and the insurance company pays the remaining $1500. Coverage limits are also crucial; they define the maximum amount the insurance company will pay for a single claim or a specific period. Knowing these terms helps you understand your responsibilities and what you can expect from your insurer when you make a claim.

Choosing the Right Insurance

Picking the right insurance is about more than finding the cheapest option. It's about finding the coverage that best matches your needs. Start by evaluating what risks you face. For example, if you're a photographer, you might want insurance covering your camera equipment. If you drive regularly, you'll need comprehensive auto insurance that covers not just accidents but also theft and damage from non-collision-related mishaps. When comparing policies, consider the premiums, deductibles, and coverage details. What exactly does the policy cover? Are there any exclusions? How easy is it to make a claim? These are all critical factors to consider. Also, check out insurance company reviews to see how they handle claims. After all, the last thing you want is to fight for coverage when you need it the most.

Understanding and managing insurance isn't just another chore on your path to adulthood; it's a fundamental aspect of financial literacy that empowers you to make informed decisions and protect your assets. As you navigate these waters, remember that the right insurance can be a reliable ally against life's uncertainties, providing security and stability as you explore all your future has in store. So take the time to learn about your options and choose wisely, it's an investment in your peace of mind.

7.3 Planning for College: Saving Strategies and Financial Aid

Thinking about college can be as thrilling as it is nerve-wracking, especially when you start considering the costs involved. Tuition, room and board, textbooks—it all adds up, and sometimes it feels like you're staring up at a financial mountain. But here's the thing: climbing this mountain isn't about making a leap to the top; it's about taking smart, calculated steps, starting now. Early planning for college costs can make this mountain seem more like a hill and open up more pathways to reach the summit.

Let's break it down. College expenses stretch beyond just tuition; they include room and board, which covers your living expenses and can sometimes cost nearly as much as your tuition fee. Then there are textbooks, lab fees, and cash for your daily living. Each of these needs to be planned for. Think of your college budget as a pie chart, with each slice representing a different expense category. Some slices might be bigger than others, but all are crucial for a balanced college experience.

How about filling up that college fund pie? There are several ways to save for college, and one popular method is through 529 plans. These savings plans are not just tax-advantaged, they're designed specifically for education savings. Parents can start one of these plans, and so can you. The money in a 529 plan can be used for tuition and other qualified expenses, like textbooks and room and board. However, like anything, 529 plans have their limitations. They're fantastic for saving large amounts over time. Still, the funds must be used for educational purposes to reap the tax benefits. So, if your plans change, your 529 plan might suddenly feel restrictive.

In addition to 529 plans, regular savings accounts or even CDs (Certificates of Deposit) can be included in your saving strategy. These options are less restrictive regarding usage, providing more flexibility if you take a gap year or pursue a path outside the traditional college. Diversifying your savings approach allows you to adapt to changes in your plans without losing the financial ground you've gained.

Let's talk about financial aid—a lifeline for many students. Financial aid can include grants, scholarships, loans, and work-study programs. Each has its own application process and criteria. Scholarships and grants are like the financial aid holy grail because they don't need to be repaid. They can be based on academic merit and specific talents to financial need. Start searching for scholarships early, there are countless out there, and the more you apply, the better your chances.

Loans, while less appealing due to repayment requirements, are a reality for many. As previously mentioned, Federal student loans often offer lower interest rates and flexible repayment options that private loans might not offer. Work-study programs offer a way to earn money while attending school and can be part of your financial aid package. Understanding the nuances of each type of aid can significantly affect your college funding strategy, so it's worth delving into the details as early as possible.

Lastly, many overlook budgeting for college life until they're packing their bags for dorms. Creating a budget for your college years is more than just figuring out how to pay tuition; it's also about learning to manage day-to-day expenses. Start practicing now by setting a budget for your personal expenses and sticking to it. Include everything from your morning coffee to your streaming service subscriptions. Getting a handle on these everyday expenses now can make the transition to budgeting on a college campus much smoother.

Overall, financial preparation for college is a multifaceted process involving saving, understanding the landscape of financial aid, and learning to budget effectively. By taking the time now to plan and understand these elements, you're setting yourself up not just for college but for financial skills that will benefit you well beyond your university years.

7.4 Retirement Planning for Teens: It's Not Too Early to Start

Believe it or not, considering retirement while you're still in your teens isn't just for the ultra-planners. It's actually a smart move that can set you up for a more secure and comfortable future. Now, retirement might seem like a million light-years away, but starting early has some pretty incredible benefits, particularly thanks to compound interest, which we discussed in previous chapters. When you save money now, it will grow over time and multiply thanks to the interest it earns. This interest then earns more; this cycle continues, exponentially increasing your initial savings. By starting now, you're giving your money the maximum amount of time to grow, which can turn even modest savings into a substantial sum by the time you retire.

Let's talk about where to put that money. As a teen, you have some cool retirement account options specifically designed to grow your savings tax-efficiently. Two popular types are Roth IRAs and traditional IRAs. Here's the scoop: with a Roth IRA, you contribute money that's already been taxed (like the money you earn from a part-time job), and when you withdraw it during retirement, you don't have to pay any taxes on it not even on the interest it has earned over the years. This is beneficial because you're likely to be in a lower tax bracket now than you will be later when you're working full-time. A traditional IRA, on the other hand, involves putting in money before it's taxed (meaning you could get a tax deduction now), but you'll pay taxes when you take the money out during retirement.

Both options have perks, and the best choice depends on your current and expected financial situation. What's great is that you can contribute to these accounts from any money you earn from mowing lawns to a summer internship. The key is consistency. Even small amounts can add up big time. Think about contributing a set amount regularly, maybe monthly or just a few times a year. Most retirement accounts have rules about how much you can contribute each year and penalties for taking money out early, so make sure to check those details and plan your contributions accordingly.

Setting long-term financial goals for retirement might seem daunting, but it's like setting any other goal. Start by imagining what you want your retirement to look like. Do you dream of traveling the world, starting a passion project, or relaxing at a beach house? Whatever your vision, estimate how much money you'll need to fund this lifestyle. Tools like retirement calculators can help project how much you need to save to reach your goals. Balancing these long-term goals with your short-term needs can be tricky, but it's all about priorities. You could allocate a smaller portion of your savings to retirement now while focusing on more immediate goals like college or buying a car and increasing your contributions as your earning power grows.

Understanding and starting retirement planning this early helps you make informed decisions about your finances from a young age. It empowers you to take control of your financial future. It ensures that when the time comes, you'll have the freedom to enjoy your retirement years without financial stress. So, dive into exploring these options, set up a retirement account, and start contributing—it's a move you will thank yourself for when you are older.

7.5 Estate Planning Basics: Understanding Wills and Trusts

Let's switch gears and dive into a topic that might seem way off on the horizon—estate planning. You might be wondering, "Why should I think about this now?" Here's the thing: estate planning isn't just for the wealthy or older people. It's about taking control and deciding what happens to the things you care about when you're no longer around. Whether it's your cherished guitar, savings, or even digital assets like your social media accounts, having a plan ensures that your wishes are respected, and your loved ones are taken care of.

What is Estate Planning?

Estate planning is arranging who will receive your assets when you're gone. It's about making sure there's a clear plan for your belongings and financial savings, and even decisions about your personal care if you cannot make those decisions yourself. Think of it as a roadmap that outlines what you want to happen after you're gone, providing guidance to your loved ones and preventing unnecessary stress or conflict. Starting this planning early, even in your teens, is smart because it encourages you to think about your values and the legacy you want to leave. Plus, it can always be updated as your life and circumstances change.

Basics of Wills

A will is a legal document that spells out what you wish regarding the distribution of your assets and the care of any minors in your family. It's like a detailed letter that only gets opened after you're gone, telling people what you want to happen with your stuff. Everyone's will look different because it reflects personal circumstances and desires. At its core, a will should clearly state who you are, include a statement that you're of sound mind, specify how you want your assets divided, and mention a guardian if you have younger siblings or plan to have kids. It should also appoint an executor, the person you choose, to ensure your wishes are carried out. While you might not think you have enough assets to worry about right now, starting a will can be a good practice in responsibility and become crucial as you accumulate more assets.

Introduction to Trusts

While wills handle your affairs after you pass, trust can be effective during and after your lifetime. Think of a trust as a legal container that holds your assets—money, properties, or investments—with instructions on when and how these assets pass on to people you've chosen, called beneficiaries. Trusts come in different types, but they all share the benefit of providing control over how your assets are used and distributed. For example, if you create a trust, you could specify that the money inside is only used for education expenses or is distributed when the beneficiaries reach a certain age. Trusts help reduce estate taxes and offer protection from creditors and legal judgments, which might not be on your radar but can be incredibly valuable as your financial world expands.

Legal Considerations

Now, setting up a will or trust sounds like grown-up territory, and it is. There are legal nuances to consider, such as ensuring these documents are valid and enforceable in your state. That's why seeking professional advice is important. You should speak to a lawyer specializing in estate planning who can help you navigate these waters, ensuring that your documents are legally sound and accurately reflect your wishes. They can guide you on state-specific rules that vary widely and help you understand complex issues like taxes and inheritance laws. While it might be tempting to go the DIY route with online templates, professional guidance is valuable—it ensures that what you set up is effective and tailored to your unique needs.

So, even though you're young, starting to think about estate planning is a proactive step toward taking complete control of your financial and personal matters. It's about planning for the future, no matter how far off it might seem. By setting up a will or trust now, you're ensuring that your decisions about your assets, care, and legacy are made on your terms. Plus, it's a great way to start a conversation with your loved ones about values and intentions, ensuring that when the time comes, they know exactly what you want and can honor your wishes without added stress or uncertainty.

7.6 Financial Planning for Life's Major Events

Life is a rollercoaster of big moments—like getting married, buying your first home, or even starting a family. These events are exciting, but they also have huge financial implications that can feel a bit overwhelming. Let's demystify this a bit. Think of these events not just as personal milestones but also as financial turning points. Planning for them means more than just dreaming about the perfect wedding or the ideal home—it involves strategic financial planning to ensure you can enjoy these moments without unnecessary stress.

Anticipating Major Life Events

First things first, recognizing the financial impacts of these major life events is key. For instance, marriage isn't just a romantic commitment; it's a financial union. This could mean combining two incomes, leading to a better credit score and easier loan approvals. Still, it also involves shared responsibilities for debts and expenses. Homeownership, on the other hand, is often the largest purchase you'll ever make, involving not just the initial cost but ongoing maintenance expenses and property taxes. Should you think about starting a family, you'll need to consider everything from the medical costs of childbirth to long-term expenses like education. Each life event requires a different financial approach, but starting early and planning ahead can make a huge difference.

Financial Strategies for Major Events

So, how do you financially prepare for these big moments? Start by setting clear personal financial goals specific to each event. If you plan to buy a house, figure out how much you need for a down payment and start saving towards that. Tools like high-yield savings or investment accounts can help your savings grow faster. For a wedding, creating a dedicated wedding fund where you contribute regularly can help you manage expenses without going into debt. And for family planning, consider health insurance plans that cover maternity and childcare, and start an education fund for your future children.

Investing can also play a big part in your strategy. If you have a longer timeline before these events, consider investing in stocks or mutual funds, which offer the potential for higher returns. Just be mindful of the risks and diversify your investments to cushion against market volatility. Insurance is another crucial element—life insurance, for example, can provide financial security for your family in any unforeseen circumstances. And don't forget about an emergency fund. Life's twists and turns can be unpredictable, and having a way to cushion the blow financially can help you handle unexpected costs without derailing your plans for major life events.

Adjusting Financial Plans

Your life isn't static, and neither should your financial plan be. Your financial situation might also change as you move closer to these major life events. You could get a new job with a higher salary or face unexpected expenses that could affect your savings goals. Revisiting and adjusting your financial plans regularly to reflect your current circumstances is essential. This might mean reallocating your investments, adjusting your savings targets, or even postponing a major purchase to prioritize more immediate financial needs. What matters is that you stay flexible and make informed decisions that work in tandem with your evolving financial landscape.

Stress Management and Financial Decisions

Lastly, let's touch on managing stress related to these big financial decisions. It's normal to feel overwhelmed when dealing with large sums of money and significant life changes. One way to manage this stress is to break down your financial goals into smaller, manageable steps. This makes the process seem less daunting and provides clear direction and achievable milestones. Stay organized—use budgeting tools or apps to keep track of your finances and see your progress. And remember, it's okay to seek help. If you consult with a financial advisor, they can provide professional insights and guidance tailored to your needs, helping you confidently navigate these significant life decisions.

Handling the financial aspects of major life events with wisdom ensures that these milestones remain joyful and not stressful. By anticipating the costs, employing strategic saving and investing, adjusting plans as life evolves, and managing the associated stress, you set the stage for a financially sound and fulfilling life. These efforts secure your immediate needs and build a robust financial foundation supporting your long-term dreams.

As we close this chapter on navigating life's significant events, remember that each decision you make builds upon the last, shaping your financial future. Up next, we'll explore how to maintain and manage your wealth, ensuring that you grow, protect, and sustain your assets through all seasons of life.

Chapter8:
Empowering Personal
Financial Planning.

How exciting! Imagine standing at the starting line of perhaps the most exciting race of your life; your journey to financial independence. It's not just about getting off to a fast start, it's also about keeping up the pace, finding the best routes and navigating obstacles like a pro. This chapter is about turning your financial dreams into achievable realities. I'm here to be your coach and cheer you on every step of the way.

How exciting! Just think you are at the starting line of what could be the most thrilling race of your life; your journey towards financial independence. It's not just about speeding off to a quick start but about pacing yourself, finding the best routes, and navigating obstacles like a pro. This chapter is about transforming your financial dreams into achievable realities. I'm here to be your coach, cheering you on every step of the way.

8.1 Financial Goal Setting and Achieving: Making Your Dreams a Reality

Strategic Goal Setting

Let's kick things off by setting goals, not just any goals—SMART goals. Remember these: SMART stands for Specific, Measurable, Achievable, Relevant, and Time-bound. This method isn't just some fancy acronym; it's a powerful tool to clarify your aspirations and use your time and resources to focus your efforts on achieving your goal.

For instance, saying, "I want to save money," is a good start, but it's a bit like saying, "I want to be healthy." It's a great sentiment, but how do you know when you've achieved it?

Creating a Financial Action Plan

Now that you have your SMART goal, how do you get there? By breaking it down into actionable steps. This is where we build a bridge between our dreams and reality. Start by mapping out each step needed to reach your goal. If you aim to save $500 in six months, your first step might be to open a savings account specifically for your laptop fund. Next, set up an automatic transfer of $85 to this account right after each paycheck. Then, monitor your progress each month, which keeps you on track and gives you a motivational boost.

Let's add an interactive element here to make things interesting. Create a savings tracker in your journal or use a budgeting app to visualize your progress with charts and graphs. Watching your savings grow can be incredibly satisfying and motivating!

Utilizing Financial Tools

In today's digital age, various tools are available to help you manage your finances efficiently. Start by downloading apps like Monefy or YNAB, tracking your savings, and managing your budget. These tools often come with features like goal trackers and alerts that notify you when you're close to reaching your goal or about to overspend in a category. Use these tools to stay disciplined and focused, turning the sometimes-daunting task of financial management into a more streamlined and stress-free process.

Overcoming Obstacles

Even the best-laid plans encounter roadblocks. An unexpected expense may pop up, or perhaps you find it harder to cut back on certain types of spending. It's normal, and it's okay. The key is to adjust and move forward, not give up. If you hit a snag, review your plan. You may need to change your monthly savings amount, or you can extend your timeline a bit.

Remember, flexibility is a part of financial planning. If you're stuck, feel free to seek advice from someone more experienced, like a parent, a teacher, or even a financial advisor at your bank. They can offer you practical advice and a different perspective to help you overcome your hurdles.

This step-by-step approach to achieving your financial goals isn't just about buying things or having money in the bank; it's about learning to make thoughtful decisions, planning ahead, and adapting to challenges. These skills are invaluable for financial success and life. So, set those goals, break them down, harness the tools, and be ready to tackle the obstacles. You're not just saving money but building a foundation for future success.

8.2 Money and Relationships: Managing Finances with Friends and Family

Regarding friendships and money, things can sometimes get tricky. Whether it's deciding who pays for the pizza on game night or feeling the pressure to chip in more than you can afford on a group gift, money can sometimes put a strain on even the strongest friendships. That's why setting and respecting financial boundaries is super important. Think of it as drawing a clear map of where your money responsibilities start and where they end, ensuring everyone knows and respects the borders.

For example, if you're heading out with friends, be upfront about your spending limit for the evening. It's okay to say, "Hey, I'm keeping my spending to $20 tonight." More often than not, your friends will understand, and they might even share their limits, making everyone more comfortable and avoiding awkward moments when the bill comes.

Now, shifting gears to family money talks. These can feel a bit more daunting. It's one thing to discuss who bought the last round of snacks with your pals; it's another to sit down with your family and talk about college funds or car insurance. Yet, these conversations are crucial. They offer a chance to express your financial goals and concerns and to understand your family's financial picture. Start by setting a regular time to chat about money, maybe over dinner once a month. Use this time to ask questions about things you don't understand, like aspects of your family's insurance plan or why retirement savings are essential. Also, share your financial goals, like saving for a new laptop or managing your cellphone bill. These discussions can help align your family's financial habits and prevent misunderstandings.

Collaborative saving and spending is another fantastic way to strengthen your financial understanding and relationships. This is about teamwork, where you and your family or friends work together towards common financial goals. It could be a joint saving challenge with your siblings to buy a new gaming console or plan a family budget that allows for a small vacation. By working together, not only do you learn valuable money management skills, but you also build trust and cooperation among your team. Tools like shared budgeting apps can be incredibly helpful here. They allow everyone to track contributions and expenses, making the process transparent and inclusive.

Handling financial conflicts gracefully is one of the most valuable skills you can learn. Disagreements over money can arise but don't have to lead to fallout. When you find yourself in a financial dispute with friends or family, try to approach the situation calmly and clearly. Actively pay attention to the other person's view and express your own views without placing blame. Seeking a compromise or a creative solution that meets everyone's core needs can often resolve conflicts. For instance, if you and your friend disagree about how much to spend on a joint project, consider alternative solutions that could reduce costs or reevaluate the project's scope to accommodate both budgets. Remember, the goal isn't just to solve the issue at hand but to strengthen the relationship for future financial interactions.

Mastering these aspects of financial interactions safeguards your money and enhances your relationships. Whether setting clear boundaries, having open conversations, collaborating on monetary goals, or resolving conflicts, these skills empower you to handle money matters confidently and carefully. So, next time you face a financial decision involving friends or family, you'll be ready to handle it with grace and savvy, ensuring that your relationships, like your finances, remain healthy and strong.

8.3 The Impact of Financial Decisions on Social Issues

When discussing spending money, it's easy to think only about what we gain personally from the transaction—like that incredible feeling when you snag the latest smartphone or a trendy pair of sneakers. Every dollar spent says a lot about your values and the world you want to live in. It's like casting a vote; where you choose to spend your money can impact broader social issues, from environmental sustainability to ethical labor practices. This isn't just about being responsible—it's about being a part of a larger movement that can drive real change.

Financial Ethics and Responsibility
Let's start with ethical investing, a concept that might sound complex but boils down to investing your money in companies that align with your values. For instance, if you have a passion for the environment, ethical investing could mean putting your money into companies prioritizing renewable energy. This form of investment has the potential to yield financial returns. It contributes to the funding of businesses looking to positively impact the world. It's a proactive approach to finance, where you can choose to support companies that are not just about profits but also principles.

Supporting local businesses is another powerful way you can make a difference. When you buy from local shops, you help keep your community vibrant and diverse and ensure that more of your money stays within your local economy, leading to job creation and higher standards of living right in your neighborhood. It's a direct way to positively influence your immediate social sphere.

Socially Responsible Spending

Now, let's discuss the power of socially responsible spending. This is all about making purchasing decisions that imagine the long-term impacts on society and the environment from products that are not ethically sourced or made by companies with responsible practices. This can change how businesses operate. For example, opting for clothes made by brands that ensure fair labor practices can help fight against exploitation in the fashion industry. Similarly, by buying from companies that use environmentally friendly practices, you're helping promote sustainability.

One way to put this into practice is to start looking at labels and researching before you buy. Check if the products are made from sustainable materials or if the company is known for treating its workers well. This might seem like a small step, but if more and more people start making these mindful choices, companies will notice and be motivated to change their practices to attract conscientious consumers like you.

Community Involvement

Your financial resources can also be a powerful tool for supporting community projects or charities. Whether you donate to a local food bank, support a community art project, or contribute to a scholarship fund, these actions can have a profound impact. Not only do they help address immediate needs in your community, but they also set an example of generosity and engagement that can inspire others to contribute.

If you're passionate about a cause, consider organizing or participating in fundraising events, such as a bake sale or a charity run. Not only do these activities raise money, but they also raise awareness about the causes that are important to you. In addition, they can encourage connection with like-minded individuals with similar values, and it can even be fun. You can also give your time to the cause you are passionate about through volunteering in events or activities at major seasonal events such as Thanksgiving.

Advocacy and Financial Activism

Finally, let's touch on financial activism. This is about using your voice and financial power to advocate for change. It could involve participating in campaigns that call for businesses to adopt more ethical practices or lobbying for financial literacy to be included in school curricula. By speaking out, you can influence consumer behavior and the policies that govern how businesses operate.

You can start by joining or forming clubs at school that focus on financial literacy and responsibility. These groups can be platforms for discussing issues, sharing information, and organizing community activities that promote responsible financial behavior. Social media can also be used as a tool for advocacy. Sharing your experiences and knowledge about ethical spending or investing can enlighten others and spread the word about financial decisions that can help shape a better society.

Every financial decision you make can reflect your values and express your power to influence the world. From what you invest in where you shop and how you advocate for change, your financial choices can contribute to societal well-being and ethical business practices. So, next time you open your wallet, think about the impact your money could have. It's not just about spending; it's about making a statement and being a part of the change, you wish to see in the world.

8.4 Staying Financially Informed: Resources and Tips for Continuous Learning

Navigating the ocean of financial information can sometimes feel like you're trying to find treasure without a map. But guess what? You're not alone on this ship, and there are plenty of tools and tricks to help you steer clear of misinformation and keep your knowledge updated as the financial seas change. Identifying reliable financial information is like learning to spot a lighthouse in a storm—it keeps you moving in the right direction. Let's break down how you can develop this critical skill.

First up, sharpening your critical thinking and fact-checking skills is crucial. In an age where information is just a click away, it's easy to come across financial advice that sounds legit but needs to be backed by solid facts. Always double-check the sources of the information you find. Is the article you're reading written by a reputable financial expert or institution? Check the credentials of the author and look for any signs of bias.

Websites ending in ".edu" or ".gov" are generally more reliable and often linked to educational or government institutions. Also, cross-reference the information with multiple sources. If you find the same advice on several respected sites, it's more likely to be trustworthy.

Now, for the fun part—exploring continuous education resources. The internet is a great place to learn and is full of learning materials that can keep you clued into the financial world. For a start, online courses on platforms like Coursera or Khan Academy offer a range of free or low-cost classes on everything from basic budgeting to advanced investing. These courses come with various learning activities, such as video lectures and quizzes, and some even have forums where discussions can take place with fellow learners. Podcasts are another great tool. Tune into shows like "So Money" or "The Financial Diet" while you're on the go. They can turn your morning commute or workout session into a mini classroom.

Blogs and books are also invaluable resources. Blogs like "Mr. Money Mustache" and "The Penny Hoarder" offer practical, easy-to-understand advice on various topics that are perfect for young investors and savers. As for books, consider classics like "Rich Dad Poor Dad" by Robert Kiyosaki or "The Richest Man in Babylon" by George S. Clason. These books provide timeless wisdom in an engaging format. They are a great way to deepen your understanding of personal finance.

Engaging with Financial Communities

Getting involved in financial communities can take your learning to the next level. Why learn alone when you can join forces with others just as eager to grow their financial knowledge? Online forums like Reddit's /personal finance or The Money Mustache Forum offer spaces where questions can be asked, and people can share their experiences and get advice from a community of novices and experts. Remember to keep a critical eye on the advice you receive here, as only some are certified experts.

Social media groups focused on personal finance can also be a goldmine of tips and support. Look for Facebook groups or LinkedIn networks where financial topics are the main focus. These platforms often host live events or webinars and host experts who can share insights and answer questions in real-time. Plus, they can be a great way to stay motivated; seeing others achieve their financial goals can be an inspiration for you to keep pushing towards your own.

Lastly, pay attention to the value of local clubs or workshops. Check if your school, community center, or local library offers clubs focused on economics, business, or personal finance. These groups often provide a hands-on learning environment where you can apply what you've learned online or in books, and they can be a fantastic way to meet mentors who can guide you through your financial journey.

Adapting to Financial Changes

Staying informed about changes in the financial world, such as new laws, economic shifts, or emerging technologies, is crucial. These changes can directly impact on your personal finances, from how you save and invest to how you prepare for taxes. Make a habit of reading financial news from credible sources or subscribing to newsletters from financial education websites. This keeps you informed about the world and helps you understand how global events can affect your financial situation.

For instance, a new tax law might change how you should file your taxes, or a sudden shift in the economy could affect your investment decisions. You will need to stay up to date so you can adjust your financial goals, accordingly, ensuring you're always aligned with the current financial landscape. This adaptability is key to maintaining and growing your wealth over time.

Keeping up with financial education is not just about protecting your money; it's about expanding your opportunities and ensuring your financial future is as bright and promising as possible. With the right tools and a commitment to continuous learning, you can navigate the complexities of personal finance with confidence and curiosity. So dive into these resources, engage with communities, and stay alert to changes. Your financial education is a lifelong adventure; every piece of knowledge you gain is a steppingstone to greater success.

8.5 Celebrating Financial Milestones: Recognizing and Rewarding Your Progress

Achieving financial goals feels fantastic. It's like hitting a high score in your favorite video game or nailing a perfect score on a tough test. But it's not just about reaching that goal—it's about recognizing and celebrating every win. Setting meaningful milestones within your financial goals can turn your journey into a series of victories, keeping your motivation high and your spirits even higher.

Let's say you're saving up for a new bike, which costs $200. Instead of seeing it as one giant leap, break it down: celebrate when you hit $50, $100, $150, and the final $200. Each milestone inches you closer to your goal and acknowledging these steps can keep you pumped and focused. You might even create a visual tracker, like a chart or a series of boxes you check off on your wall, which can be a daily reminder of your progress and a boost to keep pushing forward.

How about adding a sprinkle of fun to this process with a personal reward system? This isn't about undermining your financial goals but about enhancing the journey. For every milestone you reach, treat yourself to a small reward. It could be a movie night with friends when you save the first $50 or a small outing when you reach $100. These rewards shouldn't derail your financial plans but rather complement them. They serve as a motivational boost and make the process enjoyable. It's like giving yourself a pat on the back for a job well done. Remember, the key is to keep these treats modest; they should feel special without setting back your ultimate goal. This balance keeps your financial plan on track while celebrating your hard work and dedication.

Reflecting on your financial progress is another vital aspect of your financial journey. Consider keeping a financial journal or starting a blog where you document your savings journey, the challenges you face, and the victories you achieve along the way. This reflective practice doesn't just serve as a personal archive of your financial history; it enhances your understanding of personal finance and helps you appreciate how far you've come. Writing about your experiences can also clarify your thoughts and feelings about money, uncovering insights that might not be apparent from just looking at numbers. Plus, sharing your journey could inspire others, turning your personal story into encouragement for friends or family members struggling with their own financial goals.

Sharing your successes can magnify the joy you feel from your achievements. Don't hesitate to share that excitement with peers or family members when you reach a financial milestone. It could be a social media post, a family dinner conversation, or a chat with a friend. Sharing allows others to celebrate with you and reinforces your achievement. It's a way of solidifying the win in your mind and heart.

Furthermore, your story could inspire someone else to start their financial journey or pursue their goals. Your success thus becomes a beacon, lighting the way for others, and this shared experience can foster a supportive community around positive financial habit. Celebrate every step forward. Sharing that progress with family and friends makes the journey all the richer and more rewarding.

8.6 Preparing for Financial Autonomy: A Checklist for Teens Transitioning to Adulthood

As you get closer to adulthood, the financial landscape starts to change. It's like moving from the pool's shallow end to the deeper part—it's the same pool, but things got a lot more exciting and challenging. You need a solid set of financial skills to navigate these waters smoothly. Let's explore a checklist of these skills, why they matter, and how you can master them.

Essential Financial Skills

First up on our checklist is budgeting. If you still need to start a budget, now's the time. Understanding how to plan and control your spending according to your income is foundational. Next is saving. As simple as it sounds, saving is a discipline, and mastering it early can lead to financial freedom sooner than most people think. Investing is another key skill. Learning the basics of investing and starting small can set you up for future economic gains. Lastly, credit management is crucial. Knowing how to use credit wisely, understanding interest rates, and managing debt are all part of making sure your credit score is healthy, which will be vital for big purchases or loans in the future.

Each of these skills builds on the others. Effective budgeting can lead to more funds being available to save and invest. Good investment returns can further enhance your savings and overall financial stability. Managing credit wisely supports all these efforts by helping maintain financial flexibility without falling into debt traps.

Legal and Financial Responsibilities

As you transition into adulthood, new responsibilities will knock on your door. Understanding taxes is one of the first adult financial duties you'll encounter. Knowing how this works is essential, whether income tax from your first full-time job or sales tax on your purchases. Next is insurance—from health to auto insurance, understanding what these are for and why you need them protects you against unexpected financial shocks. Contractual obligations, like those you agree to when signing a lease or a job contract, are also part of adult life. Knowing what you agree to and what the implications are is crucial.

Navigating these responsibilities means staying informed and seeking advice when needed. Feel free to ask parents, mentors, or financial advisors for guidance. The more you know, the better prepared you'll be to handle these responsibilities wisely.

Transition Planning

Transitioning from being financially dependent to independent is like learning to drive. You start by understanding the controls and rules and then practice until it becomes second nature. Setting up your own bank accounts is a good start. This gives you control over your money and helps you establish a financial identity. Building credit is another critical step. Start with a low-limit credit card or become an authorized user on a parent's card. You can use the credit card responsibly to build your credit history.

Managing your own bills, from your cell phone to utilities if you move out, helps you understand the true cost of living independently. Each step requires careful thought and planning. Use tools like financial apps to track your expenses and credit score and create a budget that fits your income and expenses. Review your financial situation regularly and adjust your plans as needed. This proactive approach will smoothen your transition to economic independence.

Support Networks

Lastly, consider the power of a strong support network. As you transition to financial independence, having mentors, whether family members who are savvy about finances or professionals like financial advisors, can provide invaluable guidance. Peers learning about or interested in personal finance can offer support and share learning experiences. Always try to engage in discussions, share your experiences and ask questions. These networks can provide moral support, advice, and information to help you avoid common pitfalls and accelerate your learning curve.

Building these networks can be informal and accessible. Start by joining online forums or local clubs that focus on financial literacy. Attending workshops or seminars on personal finance. The relationships and knowledge you build will be key assets as you navigate the complexities of adult finances.

In wrapping up this chapter, remember that transitioning to financial independence is a significant phase in your life. It's about more than just money—it's about setting the stage for your future. By mastering essential financial skills, understanding your new responsibilities, planning carefully for your transition, and building a supportive network, you're laying down a strong foundation for a successful and independent financial future. As we close this chapter, carry forward the lessons and strategies you've learned. They are steps towards financial autonomy and stepping stones to achieving your dreams and goals in the wider world.

Conclusion

Wow, what a journey we have undertaken together! From the basics of banking, saving, and budgeting to the more complex world of investing, dealing with debt and credit, and planning for important financial milestones — we've been through a lot. Remember when we started deciphering financial jargon and drawing up our first budget? Now, you have the tools you need to navigate the more advanced areas of personal financial planning and move confidently towards financial independence.

Starting your financial education early say i.e in your teens, is like planting a seed that will grow into a strong tree. It lays the foundation for a lifetime of financial success. Think about the benefits we've discussed:

- Early investing.

- The incredible power of compounding interest.

- Developing good financial habits right from the start.

These aren't just concepts but tools for building a solid financial future. Our chapters cover basic financial skills and concepts such as budgeting, saving, spending wisely, understanding credit, and investing wisely. These are the building blocks for your financial literacy. But don't stop there. Keep building on what you've learned. Read up on financial newsletters, follow reputable blogs, participate in online forums, or attend workshops. There is a whole community ready to support you in your education.

And let's not keep all this newfound knowledge to ourselves. Talk to your friends and family about money matters. Sharing what you've learned will strengthen your understanding and can help others around you. Imagine the impact it would have if everyone in your circle of friends started making informed financial decisions!

I believe in you and your ability to take control of your financial destiny. You have the knowledge, tools, and skills to make smart financial decisions and put them to good use.

Thank you so much for joining me on this exciting journey to personal financial literacy. Your engagement and eagerness to learn have made all the difference. Remember, this isn't the end—it's just the beginning of a lifelong adventure in finance. Keep exploring, keep learning, and keep growing. And I'd love to hear from you! Share your successes, your challenges, or any questions you might have.

So, what are you waiting for? Let's take that first step towards financial independence together. Start implementing what you've learned, and watch your small steps become giant leaps toward financial freedom. Here's to your success and all the fantastic things you will achieve!

Activity: Match the term to its definition by drawing a line across

Earning	A storage unit for your cash, ideal for the money you don't plan to use right away. You earn interest for keeping your money
Savings	Buying something you need or want
Budget	Money received from offering your service e.g baby sitting or Lawn mowing
Spending	Putting money aside for a rainy day preparing and or future needs and wants.
Savings account	A game plan or blueprint for your money. It's a plan that helps you manage your money.

Find out: what is the current interest rate for your savings account?

What is your current credit score?

Activity: Match the term to its definition by drawing a line across

| Assets | Something that can grow into more money, such as when you start your own small business or put money into a savings account that grows over time. |

| Liability | What you earn when you make your money available to someone else for their use for a period. |

| Interests | The things you own that can be worth money. |

| Investment | What you owe and must pay back |

| Borrowing | Taking money from a friend to pay back later or using credit cards to purchase everyday needs and wants with a view to paying back later with or without interest |

END OF BOOK REVIEW

Title: Keeping the Journey Alive

Now that you have all the tools you need for a financially secure future through saving, budgeting, financial planning, spending, and investing, it's time to share your new knowledge and help others on their journey.

By leaving your honest opinion of this book on Amazon, you'll guide other teens to the information they need to succeed, just like you did. Your review can be the spark that inspires someone else to take control of their financial future.

Thank you for your help. *Money Skills for Teens* stays alive when we share what we've learned and you're helping me do just that.

- Click below or copy the link to a browser to leave your review on Amazon.

- https://www.amazon.com/review/review-your-purchases/?asin=B0DCC2ZJSL

- https://www.amazon.co.uk/review/review-your-purchases/?asin= B0DCLBJ92S

Other Books by This Author

Scan QR code to go to this Author's page

If you would like to know more about upcoming books by this author, please email:

K.emmanuel2024@yahoo.com

Watch out for the Author's book coming soon.

If you would like advance reader's copy of the above book, please email k.emmanuel2024@yahoo.com

Free Bonus eBook and Workbook:

Bonus one

"Teen Cash Flow: The Quick Guide to Earning Money Online and Building Multiple Income Streams"

Bonus Two

8 Days to Financial Savvy; A Step-by-Step Workbook for Setting up Teen Personal Finance

To get these for free please email: K.emmanuel2024@yahoo.com

List of Activities to complete

1. List your expenses and income and create a budget.

2. If you have no earnings, identify your earnings potential and opportunities i.e. how you can start to earn some money for yourself.

3. Open your first bank account including savings account.

4. Agree a savings plan, you can download and use an app such as Monefy.

5. Think about a savings goal you want to achieve and start a savings plan.

6. Identify an app and start making small investments. You can start by investing $10 a month or less if you cannot afford it.

7. Commit to completing these tasks and watch your personal finance take on a life of its own.

References

- *From First Paycheck to College Costs: Teen Named Financial Literacy Ambassador* https://www.bgca.org/news-stories/2023/September/from-first-paycheck-to-college-costs-teen-named-financial-literacy-ambassador/

- *The Best Money Apps for Kids and Teens* https://www.allcards.com/best-money-apps-for-kids-and-teens/

- *How to Help Teens Harness the Power of Compound Interest* https://www.firstalliancecu.com/blog/teach-teens-compound-interest#:~:text=The%20simplest%20explanation%20is%20that,which%20comes%20to%2060%20cents.

- *Budgeting for teens: 18 tips for growing your money young* https://www.creditkarma.com/financial-planning/i/budgeting-for-teens

- *23 Best Money Apps for Teens*

  https://www.kidsmoney.org/teens/money-management/apps/

- *Budgeting for Teens: Teaching Teens to Save*

  https://www.regions.com/insights/personal/personal-finances/budgeting-and-saving/teaching-teens-how-to-save-money

- *Budgeting for Young Adults: 19 Money Saving Tips for 2024*

  https://www.stash.com/learn/budgeting-for-young-adults/

- *The Impact of Social Media on Teen Spending Habits*

  https://investorscabin.com/articles/the-impact-of-social-media-on-teen-spending-habits

- *What You Need to Know About Bank Accounts for Teens*

  https://www.takechargeamerica.org/what-you-need-to-know-about-bank-accounts-for-teens/#:~:text=Find%20the%20Right%20One&text=You%20may%20choose%20to%20open,to%20cosign%20on%20the%20account.

- *The Complete Guide to Understanding Credit Scores*

  https://www.experian.com/blogs/ask-experian/credit-education/score-basics/understanding-credit-scores/

- *6 Credit Card Tips to Teach Your Teen* https://www.navyfederal.org/makingcents/credit-debt/teen-credit-card-tips.html
- *How to help prevent identity theft: 19 security tips* https://lifelock.norton.com/learn/identity-theft-resources/how-to-prevent-identity-theft
- *How to Make a Resume for Teens With Examples* https://www.mydoh.ca/learn/blog/career/how-to-make-a-resume-for-teens-with-examples/
- How to Choose the Right Bank Account for Your Needs. https://financeclap.com/choose-right-bank-for-your-needs/
- *Teenpreneur: 31 Profitable Online Side Hustles for Teens* https://www.doola.com/blog/online-side-hustles-for-teens/
- *14 Teen Entrepreneurs and How They Succeeded* https://www.oxford-royale.com/articles/14-teen-entrepreneurs/
- *How to Use TikTok for Business: A Step-by-Step Guide* https://blog.hootsuite.com/tiktok-for-business/

- *5 Apps To Help Teens Start Investing*
  https://www.forbes.com/sites/robertberger/2022/05/08/5-apps-to-help-teens-start-investing/

- *Bonds vs. Stocks: A Beginner's Guide*
  https://www.nerdwallet.com/article/investing/stocks-vs-bonds

- *Visualizing the Extraordinary Power of Compound Interest*
  https://wealth.visualcapitalist.com/visualizing-power-compound-interest/

- *Teenagers Are Pouring Into the Stock Market - WSJ*
  https://www.wsj.com/story/teenagers-are-pouring-into-the-stock-market-2d9f9fc3#:~:text=Kaida%20Benes%2C%20a%2013%2Dyear,on%20edge%20about%20potential%20losses.

- *6 Lessons to Teach Credit to Your Kids and Teens*
  https://www.capitalone.com/learn-grow/money-management/teaching-kids-about-credit/

- *Good Debt vs. Bad Debt - Britannica*
  https://www.britannica.com/money/good-debt-vs-bad-

debt#:~:text=Good%20debt%E2%80%94mortg ages%2C%20student%20loans,when%20overus ed%2C%20can%20turn%20bad.

- *Budgeting for Teens* https://www.bgca.org/news-stories/2022/May/five-tips-for-teens-to-avoid-debt/

- *What You Should Know about Student Loans - Fastweb* https://www.fastweb.com/financial-aid/articles/seven-things-high-school-students-should-know-about-student-loans

- *Teens and Income Taxes: Do They Need to File? - Investopedia* https://www.investopedia.com/teens-and-income-taxes-7152618

- *Best Health Insurance For Young Adults Of 2024* https://www.forbes.com/advisor/health-insurance/best-health-insurance-for-young-adults/

- *Savings Plans for College: 529 Plans vs. Roth IRAs* https://www.investopedia.com/529-plan-vs-roth-ira-for-college-4771260

- *How to Ease Your Kids Into Estate Planning - NerdWallet* https://www.nerdwallet.com/article/finance/kids-estate-planning

- *Apps Try Putting Financial Literacy at Kids' Fingertips* https://www.nytimes.com/2021/08/27/business/kids-financial-literacy-apps.html
- *A guide to budgeting for teens - Greenlight* https://greenlight.com/learning-center/saving/budget-for-teenagers
- *What is Ethical Consumption? Decisions for a Better Planet* https://www.transformationholdings.com/climate-change/ethical-consumption/
- *Why You Need to Learn Financial Independence in Your Teens* https://www.impraise.com/why-you-need-to-learn-financial-independence-in-your-teens/#:~:text=Mastering%20financial%20literacy%20early%20on,into%20a%20full%2Dfledged%20adult.
- Are There Any Fees or Charges to Start a Bank Account? - Burptech. https://burptech.com/are-there-any-fees-or-charges-to-start-a-bank-account/
- What Affects Credit Scores | KOHO. https://www.koho.ca/credit-building/what-affects-credit-scores/

- How to Rebuild Your Credit in 2022 | HomeFree-USA.
  https://homefreeusa.org/2022/02/24/how-to-rebuild-your-credit-in-2022/
- Banking Essentials: Top 5 Services You Can't Miss in West Lafayette, Indiana | Wizley Finance.
  https://wizelyfinance.com/banking-essentials-top-5-services-you-cant-miss-in-west-lafayette-indiana/
- How Much Does It Cost to Open a Bank Account?.
  https://www.crediful.com/how-much-does-it-cost-to-open-a-bank-account/
- The Benefits of Having a Good Credit Score | St. Johns Bank - St. Johns Bank Blog.
  https://stjohnsbank.socialjoey.com:443/post/the-benefits-of-having-a-good-credit-score-st-johns-bank/
- Which of the Following Actions Has No Impact on Your Credit Score? - commons-credit-portal.org.
  https://commons-credit-portal.org/which-of-the-following-actions-has-no-impact-on-your-credit-score/
- Which of the Following Actions Has No Impact on Your Credit Score? - commons-credit-portal.org.

- https://commons-credit-portal.org/which-of-the-following-actions-has-no-impact-on-your-credit-score/
- Happy Financial Literacy Month: Common Questions About Money. https://www.accessliving.org/newsroom/blo g/financial-literacy-is-a-step-to-financial-empowerment/
- How to use a Credit Card? | Credello. https://www.credello.com/credit-cards/how-to-use-a-credit-card/
- 5 Tips For Keeping Your Login Information Safe - SaF-Shop. https://safshop.net/keeping-login-information-safe/
- https://www.cnbc.com/2021/04/05/giving-kids-an-early-financial-education-pays-off-in-the-future.html
- Budgeting for Teens
- Meet the teenage entrepreneurs making millions - BBC News
- Child entrepreneurs turning ideas into money making businesses | A Current Affair
- Understanding Your Rights as an Employee - Shafer Leadership Academy.

https://www.shaferleadership.com/events/understanding-your-rights-as-an-employee/

- Learn The Basics of Creating Content To Grow Your Law Firm. https://www.meanpug.com/the-power-of-content-for-a-law-firm-website-tips-and-tricks/

- How can i get more followers on instagram?. https://smmmax.com/ko/blog/how-can-igetmore-followers-on-instagram

- How to Make Money on TikTok. https://greatsmm.pro/blog/how-to-make-money-ontiktok

- https://www.stlouisfed.org/open-vault/2018/september/how-compound-interest-works

- Money management: 6 tips to enhance your finances. https://www.worldexcellence.com/money-management-tips-on-how-to-manage-your-money/

- Unlock Success: Smartest Financial Decisions You Aren't Making | NewMaker Financial. https://www.newmakerfinancial.com/education-center/unlock-success-smartest-financial-decisions-you-arent-making

- Riding Towards Wealth: The Pursuit of Financial Happiness and the Wisdom of Rich Dad Poor Dad. https://www.troubadourmag.com/post/riding-towards-wealth-the-pursuit-of-financial-happiness-and-the-wisdom-of-rich-dad-poor-dad

- How Compound Interest Works & How to Estimate It. https://www.stlouisfed.org/open-vault/2018/september/how-compound-interest-works

- Millionaires are made in their 20s and 30s – Here's How - The Money Tea. https://themoneytea.com/2020/04/13/millionaires-are-made-in-their-20s-and-30s-heres-how/

- Options Trading - Beginner's Guide. https://www.gettogetherfinance.com/blog/options-trading-beginners-guide/

- How Much Should You Save For College? | College Counselor Services. https://www.collegecounselorservices.com/faq/how-much-should-you-save-for-college/

- 10 Easy Ways To Start Investing With Little Money. https://fundstask.com/10-easy-ways-to-start-investing-with-little-money/

- How to Invest 500 - Where To Invest Money. https://wheretoinvest.money/how-to-invest-500/

- Best practices for safe online browsing and avoiding phishing scam | TechRepublic. https://www.techrepublic.com/forums/discussions/what-are-best-practices-for-safe-online-browsing-and-avoiding-phishing-scam/

- Navigating Volatility – Financial Advice for Small Business Owners - RVA Small Business Network. https://rvasbn.com/featured-interviews/navigating-volatility-financial-advice-for-small-business-owners/

- Investing in Tomorrow: Actions Your Future Self Will Thank You For - Once In A Blue Moon. https://onceinabluemoon.ca/investing-in-tomorrow-actions-your-future-self-will-thank-you-for/

- Finding the Best Credit Cards for You | ScoreSense. https://www.scoresense.com/finding-best-credit-cards/

- 10 Common Credit Card Mistakes to Avoid | Capital One. https://www.capitalone.com/learn-grow/money-management/common-credit-card-mistakes-to-avoid/
- Grants for Living Expenses While in College: How to Get 2024. https://applyforcollegegrantsonline.com/grants-for-living-expenses-while-in-college/
- Top Student Loan Banks: The Ultimate Guide | Pay Day Loan. https://www.paydayloanust.com/top-student-loan-banks
- How to Maintain a Good Credit Score Today. https://kingofkash.com/blog/maintain-good-credit-score/
- Why Payday Loans Are A Bad Idea - magazinevibes.com. https://magazinevibes.com/why-payday-loans-are-a-bad-idea/
- Great Advice For Handling Your Personal Finances – Colorado Listing Agent | Sell Your Colorado Home. https://housecallsrealty.com/great-advice-for-handling-your-personal-finances/

- Bankruptcy and Your Credit Score: The Facts. https://solutions.revivefinancial.com.au/artic les/bankruptcy-and-your-credit-score-the-facts

- 8 private student loans to help you pay for college. https://www.foxla.com/money/private-student-loans

- US Income Taxes - International Center. https://icenter.tufts.edu/practical-matters/us-income-taxes/

- What is an IRA & IRA Interest Rates | Huntington Bank. https://www.huntington.com/learn/invest-retire/what-is-an-ira

- Should I Accept All of the Financial Aid Offered to Me?. https://www.sparrowfi.com/blog/should-i-accept-all-of-the-financial-aid-offered-to-me

- Costs and Aid | Undergraduate Admissions. https://www.admissions.rutgers.edu/costs-and-aid

- Traditional vs. Roth IRAs. https://blog.mycsbin.com/traditional-vs-roth-iras

- Responsible Borrowing: How to Safely and Effectively Utilise Small Loans - Urban Splatter. https://www.urbansplatter.com/2023/07/responsible-borrowing-how-to-safely-and-effectively-utilise-small-loans/
- Establish healthy relationship boundaries - Mentorits. https://www.mentorist.app/action/establishing-boundaries-for-he_519/
- Sustainable Corporate Governance Practices for 2021 - Hackstaff, Snow, Atkinson & Griess, LLC. https://www.hsaglaw.com/sustainable-corporate-governance-practices-for-2021/
- Mastering Investment Skills on a Budget: A Guide to Free Online Resources. https://tu.tv/2023/08/mastering-investment-skills-on-budget.html
- Why you need Financial Education? A long appeal to you, from Hubble.. https://www.myhubble.money/blog/why-you-need-financial-education-a-long-appeal-to-you-from-hubble
- How To Organize Goals? - WeeklyDig. https://weeklydig.com/personal-dev/goal-set/organize-goals/

- Mastering Money Management- 8 Tips to Management Money | Mind Map - EdrawMind. https://www.edrawmind.com/mind-maps/template/35515

Made in United States
Orlando, FL
08 April 2025

60310210R00115